Roy Lanchester has been a motoring journalist for over 37 years, during which time he has tested hundreds of new cars up to and over the limit. He has written for many outlets, including Your Yorkshire, The Examiner and The Harrogate Herald, and is a multiple winner of the Yorkshire Auto Writers' prestigious Golden Minibar award. He has three ex-wives and currently lives alone in Harrogate.

# HOW TO BE A MOTORING JOURNALIST

ROY LANCHESTER

ISBN: 9781980590248

sniffpetrol.com

For Marie

# CONTENTS

# INTRODUCTION

My name is Roy Lanchester and I am a motoring journalist. Even after 37 years in this business, it still feels good to say that because to be a writer on all matters motoring is to be given a job of such importance and magnitude that it cannot be understated.

Motoring writers are sometimes referred to as 'muttering rotters' because 'motoring' sounds like 'muttering' and 'writer' sounds like 'rotter', which is a 1950s word for 'twat'. However, there is no joking about the job that we do. I don't wish to be pompous about it, but I have to state that motoring journalists are guardians of the truth, trusted sentinels, respected guides and faithful allies, leading consumers through the murky minefields of the biggest and most important purchase that all of us will make in our lives, apart from our house and our ill-advised investment in a meat processing centre.

Motoring writers are not only journalists; we are experts and entertainers, carefully placing the reader behind the wheel of a car, and perhaps in the passenger seat if it's after lunch or if the reader has lost his licence again for reasons we won't go into. Yes, the job of a motoring journalist is far more than simply driving around in other people's expensive cars. You also have to write about them and, sometimes, sit through extremely long technical presentations, which are the very definition of dry in at least two senses. It's a job I have been proud to call my own for almost four decades, notwithstanding a short break in the early 2000s when I was working abroad on a different project.

Over the course of my career, which I hasten to add is still ongoing, so don't bother calling any of my outlets and asking if there's a job going, I have written for a great many publications and, latterly, websites, including local papers such as The Harrogate Herald, nationals like as The Examiner, online portholes including burlyman.com and specialist magazines such as Canalling Magazine. For some years, my work has also been syndicated on a small website called Sniff Petrol, and it was someone from this organisation who, in 2017, suggested that I put together some reminiscences from my long and varied career, and perhaps use them to share some wisdom about this profession I am still allowed to be a part of, at least until the hearing. I liked this suggestion a lot, especially as this seemed a fine time to cast a sideways glance backwards, it being the year of my 60th birthday and, therefore, the time I would retire if I was lazy or a woman, which I am not, despite what my GP says.

So, read on to discover a little about me, Roy Lanchester, and a lot about the business of being a motoring journalist, from how to review a car and the key things to remember when writing about motoring to an encounter with Jeremy Clarkson and the reason why I'm banned from at least one major hotel chain. It's all in here! So, buckle up because it's going to be a bumpy ride and we're probably not stopping, unless it's lunchtime or I need a piss!

# 1. IN THE BEGINNING

I was born Roymond Ernest Lanchester in Harrogate, North Yorkshire in 1957. It was a halcyon year for many reasons; petrol rationing ended after the Suez crisis; Britain tested its first hydrogen bomb in the Pacific; John Lennon and Paul McCartney met for the first time; Prime Minister Harold Macmillan told Britons they had "never had it so good"; the Jodrell Bank radio telescope became operational; the 1956 Sexual Offences Act became law; the Windscale nuclear power plant caught fire, releasing a substantial quantity of radioactive contamination into the air; and the first issue of Which? magazine was published. Quite a time to suddenly become alive, as I did after emerging from within my mother. Don't worry, I will keep all this as brief as possible, as I'm sure you find the early stuff in memoires and biographies extremely tedious and tend to skip past it, as I do. I was once asked to review a book on Mini designer Alec Issigonis, for example, and skimmed the first few chapters so quickly that it was only later I discovered with some disappointment that he was technically a Greek. Anyway, back to me…

My father, Harry, worked in the print industry and travelled a lot to various newspaper and book printing businesses across the country. My mother, Lillian, was a woman. The pair had intended to Christen me 'Raymond', but my father was famed for his erratic handwriting and, at the registration of my birth, he handed the council official a piece of paper with my proposed names on it that caused some misunderstanding, possibly as a result of his poor penmanship or possibly because, in my experience, council officials tend to be lazy, incompetent and liable to side with your neighbour in a dispute about a collapsed car port. Anyway, my father apparently "couldn't be bothered" to correct the mix-up, so Roymond it was, and 'Roy' for short. It's a name I rapidly grew into, especially once I decided to grow a moustache.

I was a large and hungry baby, and my mother always claimed this was instrumental in my parents' decision to make me an only child, a decision I was only too happy to go along with. Mine was a largely happy childhood. My father was away a lot, traversing the country in the course of his work, and I spent most of my home time in the company of my mother, who was unobtrusive, largely did as requested and, I remember, used to cook a pretty cracking Barnsley chop, although, in fairness, it's pretty hard to make a mess of one.

Younger readers may find this hard to believe, but back when I was growing up in the 1960s, there was no email to speak of. We did have text messages, but they were called 'letters' and they often took a long time to 'transmit' because the 'network' was a grumpy man called Sid who was later sacked after he got caught stealing mucky magazines from the post. For this reason, we sometimes didn't hear from my father for days or even weeks on end. There were telephones of course, but they were not the mobile kind and, as he explained to us many times, most of the places he was visiting didn't have them, so it was hard for him to keep in touch. We had no idea when he would come home until he strode through the front door of an evening, placed his hat on the hook by the barometer (in those days, hats were worn by respectable businessmen, rather than just old folk and idiots in Citroën Saxos) and then sent me to my room so that he could have a robust debate with my mother about matters such as where he had been and what he now smelt of.

I often hoped that, when my father returned from one of his business trips, he would bring me a present from his travels to exotic sounding places such as 'Hemel Hempstead' and 'Stoke-on-Trent', but he never did. My mother was more compliant with my requests and, in my father's frequent absences, would bestow upon me whatever I asked for, which was mostly food. However, whenever we took a trip into town of a Saturday, we would pass my favourite shop in the whole world, after The Pasty Kabin. I'm talking, of course, about Blue Balloon, the biggest toy shop in town. I say biggest, but it was actually pretty small and, if I'm honest, their stock levels were pretty pathetic in some areas, but when I pointed this out to the owner, Mr Sidely, he clipped me round the ear, which would probably count as assault these days! Still, no harm done, especially as he died of a heart attack in 1971! Anyway, my mother would happily allow me to enter Blue Balloon and choose a toy for myself from their shelves. There were teddy bears and trains and spinning tops but, in truth, I only had eyes for one thing – aeroplanes!

I don't know where this obsession with aircraft came from, but by the age of five, I could already identify my favourite flying machines, these being the sleek and glorious British arsenal designed and built to see off the threat of Communism from the USSR. There was the noble Vickers-Armstrongs Valiant with its unusual mid-mounted tailplanes, the huge Handley Page Victor with its distinctive fared-in engine intakes, the glorious Avro Vulcan with its vast delta wings and, my very favourite, the sleek, stub-winged, hugely powerful English Electric/BAC Lightning fighter/interceptor.

In my childhood, everyone lived in fear of the vile Ruskies dropping a bomb on our heads, yet, with this fleet of aeroplanes on our side, I felt confident they would never pierce our bulldog defences and unleash their filthy Commie nukes upon Harrogate! I can still remember at the age of eight being taken to the air show at RAF Huntingly by my father, in the company of a lady we collected on the way, whom I was told to refer to as 'Auntie Sue' and not to mention to my mother. My youthful neck almost snapped clean off as I craned to watch displays of these incredible pieces of British engineering, the highlights being the thunderous howls of the Vulcan and the ear-splitting roar of the Lightning. Little wonder that, by this point, I had made my mother take me to Blue Balloon on a regular basis to buy every model they had of these sensational planes, which I would play with and study at length, knowing that, one day, I would become an RAF pilot!

When I was aged 12, however, my life took an unexpected turn when we discovered that my father hadn't really been away all the time with business and that he had another family in Huddersfield. I remember being tremendously annoyed about this, especially when it turned out that they had a nicer house. I was even more annoyed when his other wife (who seemed to have a bit more personality than my mother) gave him an ultimatum to choose one family or the other, and he chose them. Apparently, he found these people "less irritating", specifically referring to my half-siblings Jennifer and Alexonder. Throughout my life, I have had little contact with my half-sister and half-brother, an amount reduced to a court-mandated 'zero' in 1991. Jenny is a midwife at Leeds General Hospital and Alex recently took delivery of a brand new Volvo XC60. I wish both of them the very best.

For me, the departure of my father had its plus sides. For one thing, my mother really stepped up her care and attention for me, which was always welcome. There was also another positive side effect because I had never especially enjoyed school and was delighted to discover that any transgression or low mark was pretty much automatically excused on account of my "troubles at home". To my mind, the teaching profession has always been a hotbed of woolly headed left-wing thinking, and this was particularly true in the late sixties when it was fashionable to be a hippy, which is basically a synonym for 'idiot'. I used this to my great advantage and, with a usefully reduced workload, I was able to devote more of my time to things I actually enjoyed, such as reading the aeroplane books and magazines like the wonderful Air Gazette, which I would get my mother to go into town to buy. Unfortunately, when it came to taking my O-levels some four years after my father's departure, the exam boards of the early seventies turned out not to be such joss stick-smoking softies and my results were best described as 'not very good'. My mother was, of course, distraught and expressed her concern in the usual manner by spending the afternoon weeping in the lounge with the curtains drawn. I, however, was less concerned. Frankly, I couldn't wait to see the back of Grebe Fields Secondary Modern School as I, Roymond Ernest Lanchester, was going to become a fighter pilot!

Having finished school, I found myself extremely busy with other matters, such as hanging around with my old schoolmates, smoking cigarettes in the park and all the other fashionable pastimes in that warm summer of 1973. I was, however, slightly annoyed to discover that most of my school pals planned to go back to some kind of education once the summer holidays were over and this reminded me that I had better crack on with my plans to join the RAF! I would certainly show them when I zoomed loudly over their stupid sixth form colleges and Industry Training Board apprenticeship schemes in my shiny BAC Lightning! To this end, one warm July day, I caught the train to Leeds and found my way to the RAF recruitment office on the outskirts of the city centre, where I presented myself to the uniformed chap on the front desk and announced that I was there to become a fighter pilot. In that calm, cool way that marks out an RAF member, the chap introduced himself as Flying Officer Hugo Vest, reminded me that there was no need to salute him and then said that he needed to run through a few things. While I did not expect to be handed the keys to a BAC Lightning immediately, this tedious, form-filling procedural drag was not exactly a wonderful advertisement for the exciting, all-action RAF depicted in the recruitment adverts in Air Gazette. Furthermore, in launching his box-ticking probe into my qualifications, Fg Off. Vest alighted rather quickly upon my recent O-level results and, more specifically, how greatly they fell below the petty and needless standard applied by RAF pen pushers. As if you needed to know about English literature, geography or physics to whack two Rolls-Royce Avon engines up to maximum thrust for a high-velocity climb to intercept a Russian bomber! Nonetheless, the pedantic Vest insisted this was an issue and our conversation swiftly descended into petty squabbling about this and also about the eye testing machine, which he insisted he had asked me not to touch but which I had, nonetheless, touched and which he now claimed was "broken" as a result. Long story short, my dreams of being an RAF pilot were dashed that day for a variety of reasons, the final one being that, according to the Flying Officer, the Royal Air Force does not hire people who shout, "Well, shit off then!" across their recruitment centre lobby.

The unreasonable attitude of the RAF had spoiled my plans for the future and left me at a bit of a loose end. However, there is something about my childhood I haven't mentioned yet and have been withholding for dramatic effect. You see, as a youngster, I was not just interested in aeroplanes. I also had an interest in cars, and once I had exhausted the supply of fighters and bombers from the Blue Balloon toy shop, it was a common cry from the young Roy to demand that my mother bought me a model of a Jaguar E-Type or Triumph TR4. Likewise, if my mother was heading into town to get me the new issue of Air Gazette, I might remind her that I would also enjoy a copy of Motor or Autocar, if she hadn't already bought these for me. Where did this interest come from? Well, it certainly wasn't my father, who had very little interest in machinery of any kind, to the extent that, in 1976, he bought an Austin Allegro in a unpleasant yellow colour, like a mustardy turd of the kind one suffers after spending too long in France. However, one of his business associates, a stylish man called Len Tuttle, sometimes used to drop by our house in his E-Type Jaguar. He would smoke slim cigars and often slip me a shilling, which was the unit in which British money was measured before the meddling EU ruined it. Anyway, I remember 'Uncle Len' and his sleek sports car ignited an enthusiasm for motor cars and free money that never went away, and this would hold a big clue to my future! Of course, I didn't realise this at the time, hence my reluctant decision to follow my mother's advice and go back into full-time education. However, I knew that I wasn't suited to the world of schools and colleges with their hand-wringing lefties at the helm, as my final report from Grebe Fields had already made very clear. But then, it didn't really matter that the headmaster had described me as "lazy and entitled", because I was going to become a motoring journalist!

# 2. GETTING STARTED

"How do you become a motoring journalist?" is one of the questions I'm most frequently asked, up there with "How did you get back in?" The answer I give is the one I also used in response to other commonly asked questions, like "What the hell happened to these curtains?" That is to say, "I don't know". Although, in this case, I genuinely don't know, since there is no set path into this profession, not that I am aware of and I think I would be, especially if it was easier. Some people get in via other branches of journalism, some by official college courses, some by other means altogether. I won't repeat the stories about how one well-known national motoring writer is alleged to have got his job, save to note that he has definitely got quite soft hands and once got very huffy during the Fiat Qubo launch in 2008 when I jokingly called him a "bender".

No, there are many routes into motoring journalism, especially in the modern world where easy access to blogs and internet video channels has given a whole new generation the chance to show how little they know about anything. I cannot offer you advice in this field, though I will add that I believe the internet is a passing trend and that I would ignore anyone who says print journalism is dead, as they said the same about me on the Renault Scenic launch in 1997, and that turned out to be premature. Indeed, I'm confident that, just like me on that hotel bar floor, print will come round with a start, shout "BRONCO!" for reasons that have never been clear and then vomit onto a Frenchman's slim briefcase.

I should stress that there is no motoring journalist, alive or passed out with a very shallow heartbeat and a pale clammy appearance that should be blamed on an excessively rare steak, who would be able to give you a clear path into this world. Even if they did know, they probably wouldn't tell you about it because they already have a place on an upcoming Kia UK press launch and they don't want you sidling up and stealing it. What I can tell you, however, is how I got into this game in the hope that, perhaps, this story will inspire a future generation to wait until I retire before coming along and trying to take all the work, you cheeky shits.

My own break into journalism came after I had failed many of my O-levels, and subsequently enrolled at Knaresborough College of Knowledge to study metalwork. Don't bother copying any of this down, by the way, it's not really relevant to getting into motoring journalism. Also, they knocked down the college in the early eighties. I quickly grew tired of the metalworking course and successfully dropped out by dint of not attending any of the classes, and also by calling the admissions coordinator a "speccy tit". My mother remained unaware of this decision to cease my studies as she was wrapped up in her own project at the time, which was to buy and then drink as much gin as possible whilst sitting in the house with all the curtains drawn. These were happy times for me as I used to leave home as if going to the college and would then spend my days hanging out with some of my other educationally less-dedicated friends in the park, smoking and sipping on the finest ciders our pooled resources could afford. In fact, I was not short of a bob or two at this point, as my father had returned to my life, after a brief absence. This reappearance was brought on by his second wife and, specifically, her objection to the discovery of his third wife, as a result of which he now found himself between wives entirely and living in a small flat above the chemist on Woodhouse Parade. It was clear to me that he felt guilty about leaving my mother and me some years previous, and, indeed, about describing us as "annoying", and he sought to make amends in the most mutually acceptable way, which was to have me come round to his flat and let him give me money on the doorstep with the understanding that I wouldn't "bother" him for another week. I didn't tell my mother about this arrangement as it was only possible to talk to her in the rare moments when she wasn't crying, and mention of my father would only start her blubbing again, creating a rather vicious circle of wailing and snorting that I did not have time for. Also, if she knew I had two or three quid upon me, she might have asked to borrow some to buy more gin and, frankly, she'd had enough. Just to be clear, this isn't relevant to becoming a motoring journalist either, so don't think your only path into this business is by having a guilty father or a sad mum and spending all day sitting by the war memorial smoking JPS and throwing sticks at ducks. The more relevant bit is coming up now.

Some time after I had decided to get thrown out of college, I accidentally let this slip to my father whilst standing on his doorstep waiting for him to count out some pound notes. "Come on Roy, you're about 17 aren't you?" he said seriously. "What are you going to do with yourself?" I remember assuring my father that all would be fine. "Hmph", he snorted ruefully as he slammed the door and it was that fatherly expression of concern which rang in my ears as I stuffed the three quid into my pocket and wandered slowly towards The Black Cat because it was definitely the easiest pub in which to get an underage drink and I was planning on getting bladdered with Barry Bloodworth from school. Everything would be fine, I thought. Wouldn't it? Or would it? (n.b. These are rhetorical questions, just in case you're still taking notes on how to be a car journalist.) Even five pints of best bitter and some chips with scraps on the way home couldn't shake my father's well-timed "hmph" from my mind. What if he was about to stop giving me money? What if he found out I wasn't passing some of it on to my mother, which I had recently discovered was his somewhat unreasonable intention? Let's be honest, although she took pauses between gin and weeping to hold down a part-time job in a local florist, she was ill-equipped for a customer-facing role on account of her quiet voice and penchant for breaking down in tears and having to ask Mrs Shuttley if she could go home early. As a result, she would probably relish the chance to get her mitts on some of dad's guilt cash. The more I thought about it, the more I realised my hard-won lifestyle was in peril. Would I be forced to get a job and, if so, what would that be? After all, this was 1974. Unemployment was rife, strikes were commonplace and the loony left had occupied Downing Street. This was no time for a young man to stop getting money from his father/home-cooked meals from his mother.

Happily, the following week when I went round to my father's, he greeted me not with money but with a suggestion, although also with some money after I threatened to give my mother's solicitor his new address. Using his contacts within the print industry, he had called in a favour with a friend who worked at The Harrogate Post newspaper and arranged for me to meet them, with a view to being given a job. "Now listen", he said solemnly as he pushed a scrap of paper bearing the relevant details into my hand, "for fuck's sake, don't fuck it up you useless twat."

With those words of encouragement ringing in my ears, the following Tuesday I put on the suit my mother had bought me for Uncle Kenny's funeral and the tie she had bought me two days earlier to replace the one that got damaged at Uncle Kenny's funeral and headed into town to meet my 4:30 pm appointment with destiny. In those days, The Harrogate Post was a nightly newspaper published out of sturdy brick offices on the outskirts of town, as opposed to these days, when it is none of those things on account of having closed down. The office building was directly opposite a pub called The Barley Mow, which was a cracking boozer, although I was unable to discover this just yet as it was closed in the afternoons, because it was 1974, and also because I'd just spent all my cash on a pair of flared trousers, also because it was 1974. Instead, I proceeded directly to the Post's office to meet the person who would become my first editor. His name was Cyril Crest and he was very much a newsman of the old school, and not just because he used to smoke a lot indoors. Cyril was a journalist through and through and it used to be said that, if you cut him in half, he would bleed news, although, sadly, when they actually cut him in half, all they found was more cancer. Anyway, on this fateful day in 1974, I walked nervously into the Post's building and was led from reception to the lavatories as requested and then on to Crest's private office in the corner of the main editorial nerve centre. There were only six people working there, plus the secretary Jean, who I later discovered didn't really do any work but just talked about her cats and was one of those women whose job in any office is to be annoying, but there was a palpable buzz in the air; the buzz of finding daily news and then recording it by bashing it into a typewriter in the form of words, and also pictures, although they came through a different method in a different room.

"Ahhh, Harry Lanchester's lad", exclaimed Crest as I walked with trepidation through the open door of his office, its frosted glass marked with his name and the simple word 'editor' underneath. I remember dreaming that, one day, I too would have a door with my name and job title on it, though, in fact, this has never come to pass because people don't bother with such things these days as it's too expensive. However, I do have a brass plaque with "ROY LANCHESTER – MOANERING CHURNALIST" embossed on it, which was a jocular gift from the Yorkshire Auto Writers' Society, shortly before I was asked to leave both the group and the hotel where the fight occurred.

"Hello Mr Crest", I said as confidently as I could muster. Crest was a small man, but stocky of build and possessed a steely gaze that speared from behind his thick-framed glasses and just beneath where the front of his hair would have been if he wasn't mostly bald. In many ways, he looked like a smaller, broader Eric Morecambe, who had been to a few more lunches and had a bit more to drink. "Reet then", Crest continued, getting up and walking around his desk to shake my hand. "What 'ave you got to say for yoursen?" Yes, Crest was a classic local man, right down to his use of 'yoursen', which is Yorkshire for 'yourself', although you don't hear people say it much any more, probably because it's not widely understood and using it in front of southerners on a car launch will cause them to ask if you've "finally had a stroke". Back in the mid-seventies, such language was more commonplace, especially from a bluntly spoken chap like Cyril Crest, who really was a true Yorkshireman. He knew his mind and spoke it often, even if that meant getting banned from Yorkshire Television's late-night Speaking Freely political discussion series for saying some things about Asians.

On this day, however, the main thing on his mind was what I had to say for myself and I quickly began explaining that I needed a job because I was worried that my father was going to stop giving me money. "Quite right too, you daft bastard", barked Crest. "You young lads, you need to learn the meaning of graft", and with that, he lit a cigarette, marched out of his open office door, shouted "Terry, did you sort that bastard hospital story you soft bugger?" then stomped back into the room and slammed the door without appearing to wait for an answer. "Reet", he announced, which is a Yorkshire word for 'right'. "Let me tell you a bit about the newspaper business, young man…", which he then did, though I won't share it with you here because most of it isn't relevant any more and I'm going to use the rest of it in the next chapter.

Finally, after a lengthy lecture on newspapers and a few probing questions about my life, experience and views on Pakistanis, Crest stubbed out another cigarette and looked with a snort at his watch before announcing that it was "Just past 5. Fancy a pint?" This request was delivered with an urgency and intensity which left me in no doubt that it was the most important question of the interview, and I wasted no time in saying yes. Crest then emerged from behind his desk, grabbed his mac from the coat stand in the corner and led me through the editorial office, pausing only to inform his staff that this evening's paper looked "crap", and, with that, we walked across the road to become the evening's first customers at The Barley Mow.

"The usual, love, and whatever the lad's having", Crest coughed at the barmaid, and I was delighted when it turned out my drink choice was the same as his, a pint of Best and then another one. "Look lad", Crest said firmly after we had sat down. "I told yer father I'd see what I could do and you seem alreet, so come in next Monday and you can be us dogsbody. I'll pay you 18 pound a week." Eighteen pounds a week! That was more than my father was giving me, although obviously that income wasn't taxed. On that basis, and since I liked the no-nonsense Mr Crest and the exciting world of newspapers he had outlined to me, I was delighted to say yes to his offer of both a job and another pint!

So how does this tale of a first job at a local newspaper relate to becoming a motoring journalist in the modern world? It doesn't. Not unless you can travel back in time to 1974 and make your absent father feel bad about something. The lesson you can learn from this, however, is that you should always seize an opportunity, wherever it might come from.

All you need to do is find your Cyril Crest! But not the actual Cyril Crest. He died in 1987!

# 3. LEARNING THE ROPES

It's a sad fact that the young motoring journalists of today have no idea about the graft of the newsroom, spoilt as they are with their websites and apps and instant gratification of the modern age. They really don't know they're born, probably because their births are not on YouTubes or MySpace! At least, not that I'm aware of. These young lads (and probably lasses these days) simply don't understand the craft of news gathering and the thrill of constructing a story using nothing more than your nose, something I literally had to do after breaking both hands in a waterpark mishap on the Peugeot Partner Tepee launch in Cap Ferrat. Well, let me tell you that these youngsters with their smartphones and tablets and their mineral waters and their early nights because "we've got a flight in the morning" are a little too wet behind the ears for my tastes and whenever I hear one of them tutting as I order a nightcap or wipe my hands on a waiter, I like to remind them that I've earned my place at the table because I did it the proper way.

When I started at The Harrogate Post as office junior and general dogsbody, I was thrown into the deep end of both newspapers and a river. My new job was to help out the reporters in whatever ways they saw fit, as well as acting as general assistant, all under the watchful eye of ace editor Cyril Crest, a redoubtable man who set me on the path I followed to this day. Crest was a fearsome and no-nonsense man with a thick Yorkshire brogue which he kept on his desk and regularly threw at people who displeased him. He also had a strong local accent and I'll never forget the sound of his voice, calling one of his staff a "daft bugger" or a "soft bastard" as only a Yorkshireman can, or could in those days before the ninnies of political correctness closed down such harmless office banter and/or violence. These days, he'd probably have to say, "Excuse me Jean, would you like to discuss your feelings in a safe space?" and that simply doesn't work in a Yorkshire accent. It just sounds stupid, because it is. But I digress.

My first year at the Post was one in which I saw, learned and received a shoe to the head a lot. The days flew by in a crackle of breaking stories, anonymous tip-offs and runs to the newsagent to buy Cyril more fags. For a young apprentice to the news trade, this was heaven. There were long periods when I could sit down and do nothing, and at the end of a long day, we usually went to the pub over the road. I was very happy with everything. Cyril Crest, however, had other ideas. "Listen Lanchester", he said to me one day over a lunchtime pint in the Barley Mow. "Bosses are chewing me ear because three year ago they gave us a fund to train up new reporters and I've done nowt with it. Right ear bashing they've given us. Any road, to get the bastards off me neck, I'm sticking you into journalism college. Don't say owt, just try not to bugger it up, reet?"

With that, the next stage of my career was set. I was to become a fully fledged journalist! Under the terms of my new role, I was to become the Post's new junior reporter, while also becoming enrolled in a block release course, which would see me attend Ripon Tech (now The University of Central Ripon or some nonsense) for a total of 12 weeks to gain a proper NCTJ (National Council for the Training of Journalists), approved by the NUJ, who were the journalists' union, but the good kind of union that could help you with a legal challenge from a prominent local policeman, rather than the bad sort that was forever bullying you into standing around a brazier outside a British Leyland factory.

I was excited to become a reporter since I'd always wanted to try my hand at writing news stories and also because I knew for a fact that Bob Bottomly, the senior news reporter, used to go out 'on stories' and then stop for a couple in The Three Sheaves or go home for a nap. Yes, a reporter's life had appeal and no mistake! Of course, Bob and the other bitter old hacks in the newsroom made something of a fuss about this with all the usual gripes about "not qualified", "not able", "sleeping in the darkroom again" and so on. Happily, editor Crest had no interest in being bothered to listen to these complaints or having to advertise the training position externally, so the place at college and the promotion in the newsroom were mine, pending the investigation into who had left some urine on the darkroom floor. When that proved to be inconclusive, I was on my way to Ripon Tech, where I learned all about basic news reporting, fact checking, shorthand note-taking and the college's policy on accidentally setting fire to the common room. In parallel, I was shadowing the Post's existing reporters and I learned a great deal here, especially about how to avoid letting them give me the slip and which pubs to check if they did. As reporter Ken Lemon once muttered after I tracked him down to the snug in the Rifleman's Arms, "Bloody 'ell Lanchester, you'd make a decent investigative reporter if the only story in town is where the fook's Ken?" Lemon was a quietly spoken man of few words but with a marvellous sense of humour that would reveal itself in occasional quips and asides and wonderful pranks such as refusing to let me into his Morris 1100 because he claimed I had made it "smell like a wet rat" and forcing me to get the bus back from Knaresborough. In fact, it was Ken who coined my office nickname of 'The Lord', which he came up with because he said, "Every time I see you, I say 'Jesus Christ'!"

Between my time at the college before most of it burnt down and my lessons learnt by following the experienced reporters of the Post, I had a full and rounded education in all aspects of journalism, from following leads and interviewing victims to covering court proceedings and making sure the accounts office didn't reject your expenses because they had 'eight pints of bitter' written on them. Truth is, I learnt some things at the college but it was the time with the hacks of the newsroom that really immersed me in the craft of journalism and also a local water feature.

In the summer of 1976, I attended what was left of Ripon Tech to receive my diploma in journalism and, with that, I was now a fully fledged cub reporter! Normally, as the most junior member of the team apart from myself in my old job which I no longer had on account of qualifying, I would be assigned to all the small jobs that no one else wanted, such as weddings, funerals, local council meetings and going over the road to get the editor a lunchtime pint and a bag of scratchings because he was "too bloody busy". Happily, however, the news team was somewhat depleted, as Jan had left and Terry had been suspended for throwing a junior member of staff into a river, which meant that I was sometimes allowed out and about on to the news beat to see the real sharp end of news gathering.

The kids today just wouldn't understand it and I'm not going to turn it into an app, so they'll probably never know, but if you're still paying attention, here is what I learnt about proper journalism: First of all, it doesn't matter whether you're reviewing the new Renault Scenic 1.5 dCi or breaking a political scandal that will bring down the government, but in all branches of journalism, the important thing to remember is to get the basics right and that means the trusty old hacks' mantra of the six Ws. That is to say; who, what, why, where, when and (w)how. That last one is 'how' which doesn't normally begin with a W, hence I've had to add one in brackets. Don't blame me, I didn't come up with this. My old boss Cyril Crest used to say that it was actually the EIGHT Ws – who, what, why, when, where, how and where's me whisky? – but when I suggested this to the NUJ, they told me I was being 'fatuous' and also that someone had found my membership card in a pasty shop.

Anyway, let me demonstrate how this age-old and faultless mantra would apply to, for the sake of argument, the Renault mentioned above and how you might apply it to a typical first-drive article:

Who? – Renault
What? – The new Scenic 1.5 dCi
Why? – Well, exactly

Where? – Bradlington Manor Country Hotel

When? – Last year

How? – Not applicable

Where's me whisky? – Excellent catering and hospitality throughout, with only one cause for complaint, which was that there was a trodden-in piece of chewing gum on the terrace outside my room, which I couldn't help but notice while I was out there getting some of Mr Benson's finest 'fresh air'. I called the PR and he sent a girl from the hotel up to remove it while I waited.

I hope that explains the basics of journalism. Here are some other lessons that I learnt while a local newspaper journalist, which have stood me in good stead over the years and would, therefore, prove useful to any motoring journalist, I imagine, if they're not too busy on their PlayStations and taking ecstasy drugs to do any proper journalism.

– Don't forget to check all facts, if there's time.

– Don't forget in interviews to always get the subject's full name and age. It's awkward if you have to go back later to ask for them.

– Don't have a crap in a recently widowed lady's house, if you can help it.

– Don't forget the difference between 'on the record' and 'off the record'. The two are not the same and it matters a great deal that the distinction is made, especially if you don't want a local councillor in the reception area of your office shouting "You stupid fucking idiot" until Leslie from the picture desk calls the police.

– Don't go back to a widow's house to ask her age as this may be considered rude, especially if she believes you have left 'an unbelievable mess' in her downstairs lavatory.

– Don't forget to keep receipts.

– Don't reveal your sources and that includes making them identifiable by accidentally referring to them by their formal job title, e.g. 'chief inspector'.

– Don't forget that news reporting should be factual throughout, e.g. "Police removed Councillor Yatley from the Post's offices at around 2:30 pm" and only 'op-ed' pieces allow room for personal views, e.g. "That fat shit Yatley is an embarrassment to the council, and also the Freemasons."

– Don't upset the sub-editors, as they are the ones who prepare your words for print and they can save you from basic mistakes like "'Yatley is a liability', admitted one anonymous source. The chief inspector went on to confirm that no charges would be pressed at this time."

– Don't eat a corned beef sandwich in the press box of the courtroom, as some magistrates get unreasonably huffy about this.

– Don't piss off your editor by, for example, posting copy late or not owning up to your mistakes, and don't piss off your deputy editor by, for example, accidentally leaving a bag of chops on the back seat of his Ford Cortina on a really hot day and then insisting to him that the smell is "fine" as, for some reason, this will only make him more angry.

I appreciate that not all of these points are strictly relevant to motoring journalism, but more of them might apply than you think and, though my experience in newspapers may seem a long time ago, I would heed my hard-won experience very carefully, as the basics of writing to inform and/or entertain have not changed in all that time, except in several ways that we'll get onto later.

In total, I spent just over three years on The Harrogate Post, from junior reporter rising to reporter then back down to junior reporter as unfair punishment for an incident with a prominent local politician and policeman which the subs really should have sorted if they weren't in a sulk and still blaming me for the ceiling collapse the previous month, and then finally back up to reporter again. All in all, I learnt a lot about news, about writing, about which pubs would open early if you needed somewhere to 'take notes' after a busy early session in court and about who was shagging the Lady Mayoress of a neighbouring town, though I now accept that this probably shouldn't have been alluded to in a report on the agricultural show. All great lessons learnt.

During my time at The Post I also saw a great editor in action in Cyril Crest, a man who taught me two things above all. Firstly, don't try to buy new trousers on expenses just because the pair you're wearing have a lot of egg on them. And secondly, know your readership. I've saved this point until last because, in many ways, it's the most important. Crest was never more right than when he barked, "And what would the readers want to know?", just as he was never more wrong than when he knocked Jan unconscious with a shoe and suddenly 'decided' to retire shortly afterwards.

Under Crest's leadership, The Harrogate Post had a very definite sense of its readership and tailored its coverage precisely to suit it, which is why we worked to Cyril's accurately defined hierarchy of how news was reported based on local importance, as follows:

1. Harrogate
2. Places near Harrogate
3. North Yorkshire generally
4. National stories involving people from Harrogate
5. Overseas stories involving people from Harrogate
6. South Yorkshire
7. Other places
8. The south

Obviously, this doesn't really work with motoring journalism and, trust me, I've tried. It's almost impossible to get a Harrogate angle into a road test of the Citroën Xantia conducted at Les Trois Soeurs near Nantes. But the point still stands, nonetheless. There is nothing more important to remember than the idea that journalism is all about speaking to your reader. Unfortunately, in the modern age of email, it's never been easier for the reader to speak back to you, which is extremely annoying and, for example, resulted in me receiving a message this morning which called me a "useless shit". How I long for the days when complainants would have to write a letter! At least then you could take down their address from the top and poke some dog mess through their letterbox at night! Sadly, those golden days of local journalism are long gone!

In November 1979, I too was gone from the Post. Shortly after the sad and sudden departure of Cyril Crest and the promotion of his deputy, who was still moaning about the smell in his bloody Cortina, I sensed that it was time for me to make my next move and applied for a new job. Though I didn't realise it at the time because that would be strange and suggest that I had some kind of time machine, it was to become the move that put me on the path to my dream job in motoring journalism and, also, Leeds!

# 4. MOVING ON (TO LEEDS)

Cyril Crest has always taught me that a journalist should permanently keep his eyes and ears open, though, ironically, it was advice he appeared to ignore himself in 1982 when he accidentally ran over the mayor. Fortunately, I heeded his advice, which is how I came to overhear two of the other journalists at The Harrogate Post talking about a new paper that was to come into being in Leeds. Technically, I only needed my ears open for this one, but my open eyes came in handy too when I snuck over to their adjacent desks after they'd left for the evening and found a piece of paper torn out of the local NUJ newsletter, which stated that journalists were being sought for this new endeavour, along with an address and a phone number, which I copied down into my reporter's notepad with a vow to write or ring for more details. After all, this intriguing new publication could spell my way out of the Post before the sacking that at least four of my colleagues regarded as 'inevitable'.

With the address and number safely secured, my first course of action was to spill gravy on that page of my notebook. My second course of action was to 'work' late the next night, sneak over to my co-worker's desk and notice with relief that the NUJ notice was still there, enabling me to copy down the details into my new notebook, the old one having become unacceptably beefy in both smell and texture. Wasting no time, the following morning, I stepped into the phone box near the office, dialled the number I had jotted down and introduced myself to the man who answered, which was somewhat irrelevant as he ran a dry cleaner. The curse of inheriting my father's appalling handwriting. That night, I copied down the number from the NUJ paper once more, with more care this time, and, finally, the next day I got through to the right place to find myself speaking to a Scottish man called Lindis Cray. He was, he explained, the publisher of an exciting new newspaper "for the eighties" and he was looking for "bright, ambitious, energetic young journalists" to work on his new project, which would launch in the spring of 1980. "I'm your man!" I said keenly, mentally glossing over the 'energetic' requirement.

Mr Cray seemed impressed with my enthusiasm and interest, and also by the firm way in which I shouted "fuck off" at a tramp who was attempting to enter the phone box, even though I was plainly already in there and using it for its correct purpose (i.e. making a telephone call), rather than whatever he intended to do (i.e. have a piss/shoot off some illegal drugs). The good-natured conversation with Cray ended with my promise to send him my CV by post as soon as possible. This I did, and you can imagine my delight when, a few weeks later, I received a letter to my mother's house, where I was still living at the time, inviting me to Leeds for a job interview.

With no small amount of nerves, I sponged the egg marks off my suit, concealed the damage to my best tie and headed off to Leeds on the allotted day. My transport for this trip was my new pride and joy, a seven-year-old Hillman Imp, which I had bought a few months earlier, having reminded my mother that it was totally unreasonable to charge me rent as I needed the money for more interesting things. I, therefore, saved some of my salary from the Post, which finally enabled me to scrape together the £950 needed to buy the immaculate green Imp, aided by an £880 loan from my father. I was extremely proud of that little Imp and firmly believed it was the thinking man's BLMC Mini. No one could persuade me otherwise on that score, not even Jed Redburgh from school who had a Mini, nor with any argument, such as calling me a "fat tosser" on the forecourt of the garage by the council flats.

Anyway, on that fateful day in 1979, I drove my Imp down to Leeds, stopping only because the bloody throttle cable came off again just outside Dunkeswick and because I needed a shit, also near Dunkeswick. Finally, I made it to my date with destiny, which was in a new-ish office building in Leeds city centre, and called Roger Fogg. This was the man who would become my next editor, although neither of us knew it at the time as the interview had yet to begin and, frankly, because I thought my odds had worsened from the off since I had accidentally walked some faeces into Roger's office, possibly my own as the toilet break on the way down had been both hurried and in a field.

Fogg graciously overlooked this minor transgression and, aside from a rueful remark about the carpet being "brand new", he moved swiftly on to the business of finding out if I was the sort of person he wanted on his team once I'd cleaned off my shoes. The project, he explained, was to create an as-yet-untitled newspaper for the whole of Yorkshire which would, as he put it, be "fresh for the eighties". I would later come to learn that Roger loved a 'buzz phrase'. "The beating heart of the issue", "the power of truth", "what the heck are you playing at?" – he had a snappy sentence for any occasion. I would come to discover that Roger was a real straight man, by which I don't mean that he wasn't a bender, although that was also true, but that he was very serious and, if he played cricket, which, actually, he did, he would have done so with a straight bat, though I can't confirm that literally as I never saw him play. Anyway, that was all to come, but first, there was the small matter of my interview, which I believe went very well. Indeed, I left Roger's office with a spring in my step, and not just because I was worried that there was still a blob of cack on one of my shoes.

My optimism about my prospects on the mysteriously untitled newspaper were well-founded because, just a week later, my mother took a telephone message telling me that I hadn't got the job and then another message a couple of hours later saying that their preferred candidate had turned down the position and it was, therefore, mine if I wanted it, but don't worry if I didn't. I hasten to add that it took a long time to get all of this information out of my mother when I got home from The Harrogate Post's office, as she had clearly been at the Gordon's pretty hard and she was unable to get out more than a couple of words between blubbing, though, for once, it seemed to be tears and regular, unpleasant sniffs of joy. "Don't worry mum, I'm not going to move out", I counselled, but this only seemed to make her cry harder. Anyway, my booze-sodden and useless mother wasn't relevant here; the main thing was that I had a new job in the big city (of Leeds)!

I handed in my notice at the Post the very next day and was delighted when Lumsden Tildis, the miserable new editor, told me I could "bugger off in two weeks" rather than the usual four. "Tie up any stories, write that bloody apology to the chief inspector, clear your desk and piss off", he concluded with his usual charmless grunts, and, with that, he went back to reading a rival newspaper, but one about horse racing. This was tremendous news for me since my job with the new paper didn't start for a month, giving me two clear weeks of preparing for my next step in journalism by doing absolutely bugger all.

Well, a dozen lunchtimes in the pub came and went all too quickly and the next thing, it was a Monday morning and I was in my Imp making the 15-mile trip to my new office in Leeds! Almost immediately, I found working at the new, untitled paper a breath of fresh air after the stale, stuck-in-a-rut world of The Harrogate Post. It was such a relief to be a part of editorial meetings where new thoughts and ideas were welcomed, rather than greeted with the usual set-in-their-ways grumbles of "we don't do that here", "shut up Roy" or "just admit it was your piss in the darkroom". In this spirit of 'anything goes' at my new workplace, I decided to put forth a suggestion that would potentially change the course of my new career – I said that the new paper should have a motoring section. "Aye, that's a thought", admitted newly appointed deputy editor Don Ronson. "But who would write it?" Well, I had the answer to that one straight away – I would! "You've obviously thought about this one, lad", Ronson smiled. "Hmph", added editor Fogg. I liked Don more than

Roger. Roger was from the south and had a very neat hairstyle, both of which I found annoying. Don was a Yorkshireman with a friendly smile and a pipe, both of which I liked. In the face of Roger's straight-parted southern scepticism, it was agreed that we'd come back to this matter at a later date, though, to my frustration, this time never came and any attempt to raise it was swiftly shut down by Roger, perhaps because he seemed to have no interest in cars and used to walk or cycle to work from his house in Headingly. For this alone, I began to have concerns that Roger concealed Socialist tendencies that would do no one any good. We were setting up a newspaper here, not a Communist recruitment pamphlet! Anyway, there was no time to get bogged down in Roger's possibly idiotic politics, as we had a paper to launch in just a few month's time and there were many decisions to be made about style, tone, coverage, angles and, of course, the actual name of the damn thing! This last one was solved just before Christmas '79 when Roger called together the ever-expanding editorial team and announced to us that the paper was to be called Your Yorkshire. Personally, I thought it a stupid title and far too touchy-feely for my tastes. It was also bad news for picture editor Lee Beadle, who had a terrible stammer at the best of times and now couldn't say the title of his own paper without sounding like his brain had jammed again. Still, with plans for the paper coming together and the name announced, it was time for the very first Your Yorkshire Christmas party, to be held at the Union Club around the corner from the office. Roger's decision, no doubt, as he was probably keen to pop money into the coffers of his lefty brethren.

Anyway, it was at this party that I met Bernadette. She was one of the new secretaries and we had not spoken to date, though, from afar, I had already approvingly noticed her nice face and respectable breast size. Late that night, after much merriment, by which I mean drinking, we spoke at last at the bar. "Alright, I'm Bernardette", she said. "Really", I jested. "Is that the word for a small Bernard?" To my delight, she found this tremendously funny, to the extent that, shortly afterwards, she allowed me to take her back to the Your Yorkshire offices and have sexual intercourse with her. I should add that this was not my first stab at such an endeavour, even discounting the prostitute that my father had purchased for my 18th birthday in order to, as he put it, "break your duck". There was also Wendy Lemon from school who I had encountered while working at the Post because her dad was my colleague and who I had engaged in congress twice, though the second time she said I smelt of pasties, the atmosphere was rather spoilt and there was no third occasion. Bernadette was different, and not just because she had consumed a large quantity of Advocaat and we were doing it on the couch in the publisher's office. She was obviously quite experienced despite being a year younger than me and she had no qualms about taking control in quite an aggressive manner, although this might have been to do with the Advocaat rather than sexual knowledge in itself. Suffice to say, the whole experience was quite the highlight of the Christmas period for me and I looked forward to perhaps reprising the situation in the new year, minus the scratchy acrylic upholstery and smell of boozy egg.

To my sadness, when everyone returned to Your Yorkshire at the start of 1980, Bernadette gave me quite the cold shoulder and this mood continued for a few weeks until, suddenly, she sidled over and told me to meet her outside in 10 minutes, something I was happy to do but only because I didn't know what was coming. When we convened outside the building, Bernadette was direct and to the point – she was pregnant and yes, "of course it's fucking yours!" This was not how I expected things to pan out and I remember being quite irritated, not least when I remembered that the woman now carrying my child was an Irish Catholic, with all the usual bloody-mindedness this entails when it comes to seeing things through, child-wise. In fact, things only got worse when Bernadette invited me to her house that evening to "discuss the future". Unfortunately for me, her house was, in fact, not just her house but also that of her whole family, the most notable resident being her excessively Irish father who, like a lot of foreign men, struck me as needlessly emotional. My suspicions were proven to be correct over subsequent weeks and months as Kieran, for that was his name, showed himself to be one of those men forever made needlessly tearful by pathetic things like sporting events and fiddle music and rendered unnecessarily aggressive by minor problems like someone stealing the ladder from off his van or a stranger getting his unmarried daughter pregnant.

That evening, at their modest house off the York Road, was extremely unpleasant in tone and subject matter, as it became clear that the entire family wanted just one thing; for me to marry their third eldest daughter. After initially putting up some resistance, I realised I wasn't getting out of there until

I went along with their demands and so, unwillingly and under duress, I said yes.

Ours was to be a shotgun wedding you could say, not that I'm suggesting Bernadette's father owned a shotgun any more than I would say he was involved in paramilitary activity, and I kept a close eye on the latter, I can assure you. However, despite his lack of conventional weaponry (at least that I was aware of), he had access to several large hammers and was prone to fits of Irish rage, so there was no question that the wedding was happening ASAP, which indeed it did.

So it came to pass that, on Saturday 29th March 1980, Bernadette and I were married with a service at Our Lady of the Sacred Heart Church and then a reception at the Leeds Irish Centre, both of which were awful. We then moved in together at her parents' house, which was also terrible.

Fortunately, other aspects of my life were not so wretched as, in April, we launched Your Yorkshire to great acclaim and I was very proud to call myself their senior North Yorkshire news reporter, although I was later reminded that 'senior' was not technically part of my job title and I should "knock it off". Only one thing eluded me, apart from finding a way out of my arranged marriage and forthcoming fatherhood, which was my dream of writing a motoring page for the paper. Happily, within a couple of months, all that was to change and for one very simple reason, which was advertising. You see, although the paper was doing well in its first few weeks, there was a problem in the ad sales office and not because it was full of fibbing shits who wore too much cologne. The concern was that we needed to pick up more 'big-ticket' advertising from large companies that sold high-value items across the country, rather than just small companies that sold pies across Yorkshire. These desired prestige advertisers included the firms that made cars, and what better way to attract car advertising than to have a regular car page! I remember the June day this was relayed to me, as Roger Fogg and Don Ronson called me into Roger's office and explained the situation. Don did most of the talking, as Roger was probably too busy thinking about Lenin or some such. That said, he had recently commissioned a surprisingly positive feature entitled "Thatcher's Yorkshire" reflecting on the positive things the then-new PM could do for our part of the country, but I could tell that, secretly, he didn't enjoy it and was probably planning some sort of glowing interview with the awful Michael Foot. I digress, for the main point of this meeting was for Don to ask me if I could run up some ideas for a possible motoring page! "So look lad", he smiled, "do you want to have a crack at being our motoring correspondent?" Well, I didn't need to be asked twice (although actually I did because Roger coughed when Don asked the first time, which, on reflection, I think he did deliberately)! Once I had clearly heard what Don was saying, naturally I said I would be delighted! "Will he have time?" muttered Fogg, unhelpfully. "Come on Rog, there's not that much going on in North Yorkshire", Don quipped with a wry smile, and, with that, he shot me a wink and then said, "Go on lad, have a go. Come back to us in a month." Those are words I will never forget, for they would send me on a path to the career I have now.

Armed with my new brief, plus a swift reminder that a story about a new footbridge in Ripon did not require a reference to the weight of the Mayoress, I hot-footed back to my desk and began to plan for my new role. That lunchtime, I skipped my usual run to the chippy and instead went on a lightning tour of local car dealerships, gathering up brochures from which I could glean contact details for the car makers' head offices. In this one trip, I successfully scooped up literature for Ford, Vauxhall/Opel, British Leyland and Talbot, and was so pleased with my haul that I stopped for a celebratory pie and a pint on the way back to the office, usefully using the time to mentally compose the letter I would send to these car companies announcing myself as Your Yorkshire's motoring correspondent, just as soon as I got back to the office having finished my second pint. Over the following week, I began sending out my letter, marked for the attention of the press relations departments at the head offices of all the major car companies, introducing myself and requesting that I be placed on mailing lists and rosters of very important car journalists. Simultaneously, I was gathering more addresses from brochures and from advertisements and, in the case of Alfa Romeo, from the handbook of the Alfetta GTV 2000 driven by Pete Rees from ad sales who was happy to help as he was one of those people who couldn't stop talking and was probably pleased to have someone new who could pretend to listen to him.

Within just a couple of weeks, I was delighted to receive the first of many missives from car companies, it being a letter from the Ford Motor Company informing me that my message had been received and that they would be happy to include me in future mail-outs of press releases. I was beside myself with delight! This first letter was followed by many more, some personally acknowledging my new position, others merely confirming the success of my endeavours by containing a typed piece of paper informing me of an exciting new development from Fiat, Rover or Datsun, although that last one was less likely. I began to harvest these releases for information which I could turn into stories for my first prototype motoring page. As a crowning glory, I made the lead story on this trial effort an original piece of my own creation entitled "Hillman Imp – The Thinking Man's Mini", which Don Ronson later described as "passionate stuff", though he declined to run it for fear of "upsetting advertisers". I offered to tone down some of the stronger segments, such as the paragraph claiming that Mini drivers were "all women and queers like Jed Redburgh, ex-of Grebe Fields Secondary Modern School", but he felt, perhaps rightly, that the lead story for a motoring page should be a new car that our readers would find interesting.

Happily, Renault had just sent me details of the new Fuego coupe, a car that seemed to typify all that we hoped for from the 1980s, being high-technology, aerodynamic and with a plastic strip up the side. Using the information from the press release plus one of the black and white photographs provided of this sleek new Gallic sports coupe parked quite near a tree, I made this my lead and, to my delight, Don announced that it "weren't bad" and would be published in the following Thursday's paper!

The preceding Wednesday night I even stayed past 5 pm in the office just to be around when the first editions came in, all so that I could see my hard work in print. I can tell you now it did not disappoint, apart from the mis-spelling of my name in the masthead, for there I was in black and white, Roy Lanhcester [sic], motoring correspondent! For me, this was something of a turning point in my life, especially as Don readily admitted that he was "quite impressed" and I don't doubt it was he who persuaded straight-laced lefty Roger Fogg that this was a good idea. Someone must have because, by the Friday of my debut motoring effort, it had been agreed that my Thursday motoring page would become a regular fixture in the paper. I was over the moon and immediately began to plan some of the future content for the page that would increasingly take up most of my time at YY. Yes, some argued that this caused me to lose focus on my original job of reporting news in North Yorkshire and, yes, it could be argued that our initial coverage of the Boroughbridge murders was "unacceptably sloppy", but my motoring page was an immediate hit, at least as far as I was concerned. As a result, I was damned if I was going to take my eye off the ball just because a couple of teenagers had been killed and the police could have stopped it happening in the first place according to a local councillor who then disappeared in mysterious circumstances.

That glorious summer of 1980 was a happy time for me as I really got my teeth into my motoring job, and things weren't too bad at home as Bernadette and I were getting along to an acceptable degree, especially once I didn't have to see her at the office every day. Even living with her parents had become bearable as her mother became increasingly excited about the forthcoming birth and her father became less frequent in his thinly veiled threats to physically harm me.

Then, in September 1980 came an event that was to change my life forever: I was invited on the launch of the brand-new Austin miniMetro. Also, around this time, my son was born. The miniMetro launch was held in London and I was bowled over to discover that British Leyland would not only pay for my travel down to the south but would also put me up in a swanky hotel for TWO nights, so that I might be briefed upon this exciting new British car and then get to sample it for myself. As befits such an occasion, I put on my best suit, sponged off the marks from Auntie Nesta's funeral, tied my best tie and headed off to the station to be whisked to London by Mssrs British and Rail, whereupon I was met by a car that took me to the hotel where, as the confirmation letter had made clear, there was a drinks reception, followed by some informative talks and then dinner. It seems naive to say this, but I remember at the time being astonished at all these wonders and double-checking several times with company representatives to ensure that they were definitely free (which, of course, they were). During the course of the evening, I learnt that the new miniMetro had been designed on computers, that it was to be built at a newly expanded Longbridge factory using state-of-the-art robotic assembly techniques and that, having never really bothered with it before, I really liked red wine. It was truly an illuminating evening, and that was especially true of the wine, which 'illuminated' a large part of my hotel bathroom later on, and some of my bed. The following day, we were invited downstairs, where a fleet of new miniMetros was awaiting us, each containing details of an extensive test route out of London and into the famous Cotswolds, so that we could really get a feel for this world-class new supermini. In my excitement to make this trip, I discovered that I had forgotten to bring any spare clothes, but it was okay to wear my suit again because, in those days, such smart attire was quite the norm, not like today, when everyone dons sports clothes and shouts into a mobile phone. As a result, I looked much like everyone else, apart from some staining to my shirt. Even my blushes here were somewhat spared when I discovered that the branded miniMetro jumper I had been handed was mine to wear and to keep. As if this trip couldn't get any better!

My miniMetro test formed the entirety of my motoring page the following week and gave me a fascinating insight into what it was like to be invited on launches, as well as what it was like to receive a telephone call from an irate PR man screaming about a "fucking embargo". Fortunately, he left the company about six months later and his colleagues were happy to put down my transgression to youthful inexperience, meaning I could go on to enjoy British Leyland launches for some years to come! Not just British Leyland either, or whatever they were called by then, because other car companies started to invite me to their events too. Truly, I had got my feet under the table and my motoring page went from strength to strength. The ad boys in particular seemed to love it, and this gave me a lot of leeway within the paper, to the extent that I persuaded them to get someone else to cover the North Yorkshire news beat for those times when I was away testing another new car or busy reading press releases or because I couldn't be bothered to drive to Thirsk.

Sadly, things were not so rosy at home. As I mentioned earlier, my son was born in September 1980 and called Sean, a name not of my choosing and which I found, like a lot of things to do with my wife's family, excessively Irish. "Why don't we just call him Shillelagh Begorrah Guinness O'Shamrock and be done with it?" I remember jesting at the time, but this only earned me a finger in the face and a warning to "watch your loose tongue, laddy" from Bernadette's father (also excessively Irish).

Life under the same roof as her family with a small baby was not easy and came with perils I had not foreseen. For those who do not believe in post-natal depression, I can assure you that it does exist and that I suffered from it terribly. For me, the new baby was a terrible inconvenience, compromising my life in many irksome ways without giving any thanks in return and causing a great many tired arguments between myself and Bernadette and her family/neighbours. I should add that my dim view of young Sean is no reflection on the man he has become, as he is now a very handsome chap, living in Sydney, Australia with a wife, two kids and a successful IT recruitment business, though all this information is only correct as of March 2016 as, more recently, he has changed his Facebook privacy settings.

Back in 1981, however, all was not happy in my home life and there seemed to be no escape from the horrors of my home life. That is until April 1982, when I attended the launch of the Austin Ambassador and discovered something much more cheering; a motoring correspondent from a national newspaper had died.

# 5. FLEET STREET CALLS

I learnt about the death of Menzies Lusk from The Examiner on the Austin Ambassador launch at Bradlemoor Manor near Ludlow. Lusk himself was supposed to be on the event and, when he didn't arrive, we hacks assumed he had called ahead to find out which wines would be served with dinner, discovered that they did not meet his requirements and decided not to attend, as was his occasional habit. It was only when a Leyland representative telephoned his office to ask if Mr Lusk planned to be with us at some point that the bad news was relayed. The communications officer, given the nickname 'Ian Penis', though it seemed inappropriate to use it in this circumstance, gathered us together to inform of Lusk's passing when we returned from the afternoon's driving exercise. This immediately brought about a mood of great sadness among the assembled press, which was odd because only two weeks earlier I had heard at least one of the attendees describing him as a "rancorous old turd". Personally, I never had a problem with Lusk, once you accepted the impatience, rudeness, dishonesty and outright hostility for which he was known. Indeed, I was somewhat honoured to discover he would even talk to me, as he was one of the grandfathers of the motoring journalism trade and I was, at this point, a mere twenty-something whippersnapper, much younger, leaner and less prone to perspiration than I am today. In fact, it was Lusk who once gave me a piece of advice that has lived with me throughout my career. I can see him delivering it as clearly as if it was yesterday, though it was actually in late 1981 on the Fiat Strada 105 launch at Castle Combe. Lusk turned to me, tore the leg off a lobster and used it to wave to the PR representatives further down the table as he growled, "Remember son, they want you to take advantage." That scene has stayed with me forever for I soon realised his words were absolutely true, and also because they weren't serving lobster that evening and I still don't know where he got it from.

Anyway, news that Menzies Lusk had died put a dampener on the Austin Ambassador launch almost as much as the Austin Ambassador itself, which was a shame because the dinner was excellent. However, while others in attendance saw only the passing of a colleague, yours truly also saw an opportunity. While I intended no disrespect to Lusk's family, who I'm sure liked him more than most people, I had to acknowledge that his death meant an opening at one of Britain's best-selling national newspapers, one that might be filled by a man keen to get out of his current home and work circumstances because both were asking some questions about expenses that weren't going to be easy to answer.

The next day, the mood remained sombre, although that might have been because we still had some driving to do in the Austin Ambassadors, but I was concealing a mood of great optimism as I saw something at the end of the tunnel, and it wasn't the headlights of another Ambassador, which, in fairness, were surprisingly excellent. As soon as I returned to Harrogate that evening, I penned a letter to the editor of The Examiner expressing my sympathy at the passing of his motoring correspondent and respectfully offering my services in his place.

You can imagine my delight when, just a week later, I received a reply from deputy editor Kevin Leather inviting me to their Fleet Street offices the following Friday to discuss my "bold offer". It was hard to supress a tingle of excitement, even in the dampening presence of my bloody cow of a first wife, to whom I did not mention this development because she'd only tut at me or ask me to help hang out some laundry. I, Roy Lanchester, had already become a motoring journalist and now I had the opportunity make my name known in the national newspaper landscape of the infamous Fleet Street.

In fact, this was an exciting era in general, as Mrs Thatcher was living up to her Iron Lady nickname by going to war against the filthy Argies and their evil attempts to seize the Falkland Islands from their rightful owners, a conflict that would later give the mighty Avro Vulcan one last and glorious chance to roar in the face of a swarthy adversary! Immediately after the commencement of conflict proceedings in April '82, I took a hard-line stance against Argentinian corned beef, one I have pretty much maintained to this day. Those who know me will also attest to the fact that, in more recent times, I was initially suspicious of Argentine wine, although this position has softened in the last few years as some of their Malbecs are tremendous.

The Examiner, whose offices I was about to visit, took a sensibly supportive view of the Falklands War, as indeed it did of all of Mrs Thatcher's actions, and this was just another attraction for me, as I certainly couldn't bear the thought of having to write for some Trotsky-loving leftist rag where they would, no doubt, insist I tested only Ladas, Renault 4s, Citroën 2CVs with peace signs on the boot lid and the other feeble motors beloved by loony lefties of the time! Mercifully, The Examiner was robustly on the other end of the spectrum and had been since its foundation in the late 19th century as The London Examiner (the 'London' was dropped from the title in the early sixties as it obviously didn't appeal to people who hated London, i.e. the rest of the country). This was a paper I would be proud to work for, with its illustrious heritage and a proud tradition of being on the correct side of history (notwithstanding infamous editor Percival Knave and his enthusiastic coverage of Mr A. Hitler of Germany). There was, of course, just the small matter of my impending 'interview'.

Come the Friday in question, I caught the early train from Leeds to London, having told people at Your Yorkshire that I had to visit Ford's press office, as they were still trying to find out who killed all the peacocks on the Capri 2.8i launch. This was not entirely untrue, but the inquest did not require me to speak to them in person, especially as the previous week I had telephoned the head of public affairs and told him it was McKenzie Lusk who was responsible for the incident, a subterfuge based on the well-known principle that the dead cannot sue for libel or deny power sliding across a lawn and into the entire flock while drunk. With my absence from the day job explained, I got off the train at Kings Cross in good spirits and made my way by Tube and on foot and then taxi and then a few feet to the offices of The Examiner, which were in a grand old building on the legendary Fleet Street itself, and what a street that was. As I stepped from the cab, I could practically smell the newsprint in the air and I couldn't help but feel that here, in the crucible of national news, I was, at last, at home, even though, as a Yorkshireman, I didn't like London and thought it was crap. With trepidation and, yet, also excitement, I walked up the stone steps to the heavy wooden doors of The Examiner building, almost an hour early for my date with destiny. When the allotted time of 11 am came around, a secretary arrived in reception and led me upstairs through a buzzing newsroom to the large office of deputy editor Kevin Leather, who turned out to be a pugnacious Cockney man with a shock of grey hair and a ready supply of cigarettes, at least one of which always seemed to be alight and between his fingers and/or lips. "Roy Lanchester!" he said loudly as I entered the room. "I tell you what old son, you've got some brass balls, I'll give you that." I took this as a compliment and thanked him, to which he said, "Don't fucking thank me yet you prick. Now sit down and behave." I was shocked by his tone and, indeed, his unpleasant London accent, but I did as I was told as he continued speaking. "Old McKenzie isn't even cold and you're trying to nick his gig. That is some fucking manoeuvring old son, it really is. Cheeky as fuck, that's what you are, son. So why do you think I've asked you down here?" Sensing that it was my turn to speak, I replied that perhaps it was because he needed a new motoring correspondent and I was a good applicant for the job. "Good fucking applicant? We haven't even advertised the job. Fuck me." I began to think that this jellied eel quaffing lunatic had invited me here simply to shout at me and, as such, it was a completely wasted journey. After all, I could easily get shouted at in the Your Yorkshire office without having to get on a train. However, Leather wasn't done yet. "Well you're in luck, sunshine. Lusk was a cunt. And an old cunt at that. We need some new blood. How old are you? 30? 35?" I said that I was 25. "25? Fuck me, tough paper round. Well look son, I admire your bollocks. And I've got someone who wants to meet you. Come on…" And with that, he marched from his office, across the newsroom and into a dark corridor, which wound left and then right before opening out into a dimly lit chamber containing two secretaries at huge desks either side of a large door, the frosted panel of which bore a simple but impressive legend; 'Lionel Purchase – Editor'. "Is he in?", barked Leather and, without breaking stride, he received a nod from one of the women and tapped firmly upon that imposing door. "Come", came the voice from the other side and, seconds later, we were standing upon the hallowed ground of the very centre of the machine of power. There, at a vast wooden desk, below a wall of framed covers from The Examiner that might as well have been the history book of the 20th century, except that it skirted around War 2 for obvious reasons, was the man who oversaw this media titan, bald of head and tidy of moustache, master of all he surveyed. "Remember that lad who wrote in when Lusk carked it, trying to nick his job?" Leather said loudly. "Here he is. He's called Roy." Purchase looked up from his papers, illuminated by a dim lamp with a green glass shade. "Really? And what's he got to say for himself?" Lionel Purchase was well spoken in that old-fashioned way that isn't annoying, and he exuded a quiet authority in marked contrast to the noisy Bow Bells blaring of Kevin Leather. I took his last remark as my cue to do some speaking, which is what happened next. "My name is Roy Lanchester. I'm the motoring correspondent for Your Yorkshire, which is a relatively new paper covering the whole of Yorkshire, but now I've got some experience I'd like to write for a national. I think The Examiner is an excellent newspaper and it would be my honour to work for you."

Purchase looked down again at his papers and softly cleared his throat before speaking again. "Well, you're ambitious Mr Lanchester, and there's nothing wrong with that. By the amount you're perspiring, I can see that you're very nervous. There's really no need, we don't bite. Do you know how I got my start in newspapers? It was quite similar to the approach you have taken; by not taking 'no' for an answer." Purchase made a noise that might have been a laugh or maybe just some gas and then told me a little of his life story, starting in the post room at The Daily and then climbing up the ladder by pushing his way in until he got what he wanted, a technique I use regularly whenever a launch dinner turned out to be a bloody buffet.

In total, I was in Lionel Purchase's office for a mere 15 minutes, but it had a profound effect on me and I can say, without doubt, that he was the most quietly inspiring man I had ever encountered, this being some years before I was in a room with Sir Jackie Stewart. Everything about him was impressive, from his wood-panelled office to his strident views on the Chinese, and I believe he was also the reason why, shortly after our first encounter, I too decided to grow a moustache, a decision I have never regretted, even after the Nigel Mansell incident. You can, therefore, imagine my delight when Purchase concluded our enthralling chat with an assurance that

Kevin Leather would confect some sort of test to see if I was "the right material for The Examiner" but that he was "confident" I had the "correct fibre". At those words my heart stopped, although not literally, as it was some years before I came to know what that felt like!

Sure enough, upon our return to the newsroom, Leather gave me a simple brief to go away and write a 500-word piece that I felt was appropriate for The Examiner and to send it, along with some cuttings of my existing work from "that regional rag of yours", to his office within a week. With that, I bade him farewell, pausing only to establish that he was not willing to reimburse me for my train fare to London, which he was not. Happily, it was no trouble on that score since, even with the current expenses furore, I felt confident I could slip it through at Your Yorkshire using the Capri peacock slaughter story as cover. Then, it was just a matter of killing some time until my train back to Leeds, which was, predictably, delayed as, back in those days, the railway system was run by incompetent communists rather than the incompetent free-market economists of today. Finally, I got back to Bernadette's parents' house and could not resist asking my supposed wife to guess where I'd been. "The pub?" she answered flatly, as she always did. Not so, I replied, for I have been to London to seek my fortune and perhaps soon I will have a job there. "We are not going to fucking London", she answered in a tone that was hostile, even by her standards. Typically, at this point, her exceedingly Irish father entered the room and demanded an explanation for the heated exchanges, to which Bernadette shouted, "This bloody idiot's been for a job interview in London, as if we'd move down south even if he got it, which he bloody won't", and, with that, she stormed from the room, leaving me alone with the unpredictable temper of her bog-trotting dad. In fact, his tone to me was remarkably calm for once. "Roy, we're a Roman Catholic family as you know and divorce is a great sin", he said slowly. "But in this case, we're prepared to make an exception. Bernadette doesn't want you around and neither do we", and then he went into quite a lengthy assessment of my physical appearance and odour before concluding with the words, "get out of my house." Well, I didn't need asking twice, making immediately for the door, and then for another door, this one being attached to the front of The King's Arms. Some time later, I settled down for the night in the Your Yorkshire offices where, somewhat unexpectedly, I was sick on myself. It was, without question, one of the happiest nights of my life.

My happiness returned one Thursday evening three weeks later when I received a telephone call at my mother's house (where I was now living once more) informing me that I had got the job at The Examiner! Yes, Roy Lanchester was to become a national newspaper motoring correspondent! Oh, what a time it was to be alive in the middle of 1982! As well as my exciting new job, the mighty Vulcans had sent the Argies whimpering back into their corned beef caves, I was finally rid of my dreadful forced wife and the baby we had accidentally made and my moustache was coming along a treat! Of course, there was still the small matter of resigning from Your Yorkshire, which I did immediately in the hope that I could get out before the net closed in on the whole expenses issue, and, naturally, I needed to find somewhere to live down south. This latter problem was swiftly solved by tracking down an old school mate, Barry Bloodworth, who now lived and worked in the capital. I needed to move fast, so I decided that my best course of action was to cut out all the tiresome back-and-forth of letters and phone calls and simply turn up on his doorstep in the Crouch End area of north London, asking if I could stay for a couple of weeks. This he agreed to, although his fiancé seemed less keen and made some barbed remarks about their flat only having one bedroom, as awkward women are prone to do. Still, with a place to lay my head (Barry's settee), I was all set for my first day at The Examiner. Barry had stupidly chosen to live in a part of the capital with no underground station, but with a combination of buses, trains, walking and a taxi, I found my way to the Fleet Street office in time for the Monday morning editorial meeting, at which deputy editor and extremely Cockney man Kevin Leather introduced me to the attendant reporters and feature writers as "our new man for motors, and I've every confidence this one will actually do some fucking work!" I didn't expect to be dropped into the deep end like this, but I smiled and cautiously agreed that I would.

Since motoring was a once-a-week page in the paper, I was given a desk in the 'features' area of the main newsroom between theatre critic Fenton Baize and restaurant expert Joy Beavish, secretly referred to as 'Bundle of Joy' because she was fat. These new colleagues were rarely at their desks, since they were often out late 'reviewing' plays/food and they often wrote up their reviews 'at home', a trick I had yet to cotton onto. However, behind me was the lively periphery of the news desk and there was usually someone around for good-natured banter and to lend you a cigarette, as smoking back then was not only allowed at your desk, but positively encouraged.

Those first few weeks at The Examiner flew by as I settled in well to my new role and my new life in a new town without an annoying old wife. My former editor Cyril Crest was right when he once said to me, "London is a foreign place; they do things differently there, and everyone's a twat", though, in fairness, that last part wasn't entirely correct, as some of the people I encountered weren't bad at all. One in particular seemed very nice indeed. I'm referring to a junior news reporter blessed with attractively large eyes and breasts, and hair in a style known as a 'bob', which was also the man she sat next to. Her name was Marie and, though I didn't know it as I gazed upon her from across the newsroom, she was the woman who would become my next ex-wife.

That was all to come, however. First, I had to pluck up the courage to speak to her, which I did one day by sitting down at the next desk when the other Bob was at lunch, using a spurious question about the telex machine as my cover. It's fair to say we hit it off immediately and, whenever I was in the office and the other Bob vacated his seat, I would saunter over for a quick chat about fashionable issues of the day, such as the weather, the new 20 pence piece and the forthcoming introduction of a fourth television channel. Frankly, life at The Examiner and in London was good. I enjoyed working at a proper national newspaper, which contrasted markedly with being at Your Yorkshire in so many ways, including a buzz of being around people covering national and international concerns, an on-site canteen and an expenses policy that didn't seem to mind if you slipped in a couple of receipts for underpants.

Outside of work, my seven weeks at Barry Bloodworth's place had come to an end (though Barry said I might as well stay longer since his fiancé had now left him) as I had found a flat to rent near the station in East Finchley, to my mind the best of all the Finchleys and within the constituency of the blessed Prime minister, no less!

My work went from strength to strength as well, for as soon as I had started at The Examiner, I had made it my priority to telephone every PR person in my contacts book to inform them of my move. The response, I must say, was heartening and a salutary lesson in what happens when you take a step up from a fledgling regional paper to a well-established national. Suddenly, I was being invited to join some of the most senior press and public relations men in the land for dinner at some of the capital's finest eateries, initially something that made me a little nervous but which I soon settled into once it became clear that they were definitely picking up the bill. I also noticed that I moved up the queue when it came to launch invitations and that I was now offered the very finest press cars to test at my leisure. Thankfully, my new flat came with its own parking spot, and I could easily leave two or three other cars on the road if need be. Plus, I inherited Menzies Lusk's old parking space in the car park under the office, which I gather he'd punched the horse racing correspondent to get.

Another immediate benefit of my new position was that many car manufacturers sent me gifts to welcome me to my new job and it was one of these that I used in my ongoing battle to woo the fair Marie. More specifically, when Vauxhall sent me a magnum of Champagne (I presume intended as a car-name-based pun, although I never bothered to ask), I decided to offer it casually as a present to my attractive colleague, as I've never been keen on sparkling wine and find that it gives me terrible farts. Sauntering over to her desk while Bob was taking one of his legendary long and early lunches, I casually announced that had bought this for the prettiest girl in the room. "That'll be Wendy, Ron Leominster's secretary", Marie replied immediately. How I loved her impish sense of humour back then, little realising the dark and lesbionic subtext that lay beneath. "Well, I can't be arsed to walk over to Wendy's desk so you'll have to do!" I quipped and presented her with the enormous bottle, which she tentatively accepted, although I later learnt that she subsequently gave it to her sister as an engagement present, something I had no problem with since, in fairness, it was a lot of Champagne to drink on your own. The important thing was, Vauxhall's gift had given me an inexpensive method to further work my way into Marie's affections and I repeated this trick several times until I gave her what I thought was a box of chocolates sent by Girling, only to find that it was, in fact, a chocolate brake disc, at which point the game was up.

The rest of 1982 passed in a blur between important car launches such as the Volvo 760 and the Ford Sierra, the initiation of much-needed divorce proceedings from Bernadette and my regular chats with Marie whenever I was in the office. On the latter front, things were going so well that I was confident enough to seize the moment at the newsroom Christmas party, though mindful not to repeat past mistakes such as getting her knocked up after a quick shag on the publisher's settee. Such a thing would have been almost impossible anyway, since the party took place in the office and someone would have seen, though I did later hear that Pete Heaton from the sports desk fingered Ben Bird's secretary Lorraine in the photographers' store cupboard. No, my tactic with Marie was very much one of softly, softly, catchy lady and, to that end, I simply waited until she finally stopped talking to Wendy from across the office and asked her very politely if she would consider going out for a drink with me. To my absolute delight, after a little hesitation, she said yes! This was the best Christmas present I could possibly receive, surpassing even the high quality Scotch and wrist watch combo that had arrived from BL Cars. It certainly lifted my spirits during the festive period, when I was forced to return to Harrogate and spend some time with my mother (plus her irksome second husband), who I had forgotten to tell about the divorce and also the baby. Predictably, she reacted rather badly to this large amount of information at once and Christmas became very frosty in more than just a literal sense.

All this, of course, paled into insignificance during the course of the following year, for after a very successful first date at the pub by the office, Marie and I became an item! In fact, 1983 was quite the year for me between the finalising of my (first) divorce, the successful re-election of my MP, Mrs Thatcher, and the blossoming relationship between Marie and myself. I could barely believe the latter, nor indeed could several colleagues, and it seemed that there was only one logical course of action, one which I took in August 1983 upon returning from the mk5 Toyota Corolla launch at Fineston House in Hertfordshire when I asked Marie to marry me. "I suppose so", she jested in that dry way of hers that I so enjoyed at the time. Things could not have been better for me that week in '83. I was divorced, I was engaged, I had a Renault Fuego Turbo outside and I was due to attend an all-expenses-paid dinner at a fine London steakhouse with the managing director of Citroën UK. Truly, it was the best of times!

# 6. THE GOLDEN AGE OF CAR LAUNCHES

Marie and I were married in September 1983 in a small ceremony at Westminster registry office and honeymooned immediately afterwards in Biarritz, on the Datsun Stanza launch. If that sounds strange to modern ears, let me assure you that, in those days, it was perfectly normal to attend a car event with a wife, especially if it was your own. This was just one of the courtesies extended to members of the press back in this more civilised time when nothing was too much trouble and service was delivered with a smile, plus a bottle of something and perhaps a set of high quality kitchen knives to thank you for your time and to remind you of this agreeable trip every time you used one of them to open an envelope, especially if it had the car company's logo on the handle.

The 1980s were halcyon times for the car launch and I'm delighted that I was there to see and enjoy this golden age of private jet travel, fine Champagne and relatively little fuss about the damage to hotel furniture. Even the pace of everything was so much more civilised back in those days. In the modern world, a launch invitation is most likely a terse email saying that someone else has dropped out and so you can come on the UK first drive tomorrow ("but there's no overnight accommodation and please don't bring your own wine this time"), whereas back in the good old days, a launch invitation was a beautifully presented letter, personally signed by the head of PR or perhaps even the managing director and delivered to my office many weeks or months in advance so that one might carefully plan one's diary and, if a clash was discovered, politely but firmly request a helicopter to get you from one event to the other. Travel itself was taken at a more genteel pace too, with no 5 am starts or other horrors. If one was on an early flight, then one simply made it clear that one did not get up that early and that the flight must be re-booked, adding that you would still require the hotel room at the airport the evening before. These days, such a request would be met with a rude reply, whereas back then, it was simply taken care of without any need to be called a "fat piss artist".

In these heady times, flying was, of course, by private aviation or, at the very least, first class on a scheduled flight and, if this was not the case, then the motoring journalist was well within his rights to suggest that this would count badly against the model that he was about to review. You may think this sounds harsh, but it's all about attention to detail. If a car maker can't get simple things right like the booking of a plane ticket or the chilling of the wine aboard that plane, how can the journalist trust them to have engineered a reliable engine or a firmly secured steering wheel?

Conversely, I have always believed that car PRs respect attention to detail in motoring journalists, whether it's getting the name of the car right this time or telephoning ahead to check precisely which wines will be served on board the jet and helpfully suggesting some alternatives.

Of course, back in this jet-setting age, not all travel was by aeroplane. Sometimes, we might drive to continental Europe having crossed the English Channel by hovercraft, which might sound very glamourous but was, in fact, extremely noisy and with a terrible drinks service on board. Plus, one had to bear in mind that there was driving to be done upon arrival and the hovercraft company did not look kindly upon someone attempting to disembark a Talbot Tagora after four large glasses of Cabernet, as I discovered to my cost (although, actually, the cost was eventually covered by Peugeot Talbot UK, as was to be expected in those days, and I believe they kept the damaged ramp/cargo doors as souvenirs!).

Another variation on the travel theme was to be flown in high style to the overseas launch location, where you would potter about for a couple of days, enjoy a hearty dinner or two, pretend to listen to someone explaining to you about optional power steering availability and then take the keys to the model in question, which you would drive back to the UK. This was an excellent way to get to know both the car and the vineyards of France, and provided a very practical test of what it was like to cover long distances in the car, while also testing key details such as how many cases you could get in the boot. Furthermore, back in these civilised times, the car company would usually insist that you kept the car for a few days or months after you had returned home in order to get to know it in depth. One memorable example of this launch format came in 1986 when a well-known car maker flew us to Marrakech, an unusual venue for a launch but one allegedly prompted by the PR boss at the time, who was allegedly a bender and allegedly wanted to do some bumming on his alleged expenses account, I bet. To my surprise, we had a nice time in Morocco and I actually regretted complaining so much on the jet over. We were then each given a car and told to take our time getting home, which I certainly did. Better yet, when I arrived back in London the following week, I received a telephone call reminding me that the car was to be left in my company on "extended test" and that someone would be in touch to arrange collection. Having been assured that there was "no rush", I was, nonetheless, surprised to find that, some nine months later, I still had the car and I began to wonder if I should contact the well-known car company to see if they could clear the petrol receipts to date. In the end, I didn't, but I admired their relaxed attitude to this model and was shocked when their good nature evaporated, suddenly and, in my view, quite unreasonably. Looking back, it's fair to say that perhaps mistakes were made on both sides but, in fairness, I had never been told that the car was not mine to sell. Still, as the expression goes, every day's a school day, but one of those school days spent in a police station. I should add that the matter was soon smoothed over and I learnt that selling press cars for cash was a mistake and one that I would not repeat again, at least until 2002.

Of course, the good old days of launches were not just about the travel; they were also about the events themselves, and what fun they were. None of the rushing around of the modern age, the launches of the eighties heyday were thoroughly civilised affairs, typically involving at least two nights in a top quality hotel and maybe more. I seem to remember that the

Ford Sierra facelift event in 1987 actually went on for over a week before it was realised that, if we didn't get out of there, we would miss the Citroën AX first drive in Portugal!

As to what went on during those fine events, well, discretion prevents me from naming names or going into too much detail about who was caught wanking in the lifts at Chateau Mirau on the Renault 21 launch in '86, although, in fairness, he's not in the industry any more having retired from The Globe 13 years ago. Suffice to say, all manner of japes occurred in those carefree times, from the dining on the fine food and the drinking of the fine wine to the driving into the ornamental lake and the game of kicking the junior PR man down the stairs, although, in fairness, I only declared it a game after it had already happened once.

Everything was so much less serious in those days, and I think that's what made it so fun. I recall once waking a certain PR man in the middle of the night to tell him that my room was on fire and, because I had a reputation as a bit of a joker, he thought I was kidding! As I said, nothing was taken too seriously back then, although you should have seen the look on his face half an hour later when he was standing in his pyjamas in the car park desperately asking staff for the name of another hotel to accommodate everyone! Another time, I recall being in the hotel lobby after dinner and another guest making a great fuss about my trousers, or lack of them. Before this could escalate, the PR man, with consummate professionalism, sidled over to the complaining lady with the words, "Perhaps madam would consider moving to a different hotel?" and, with that, he slipped some money into her hand and ushered her towards the doors! As if that wasn't enough, he also avoided a repeat of the situation by arranging for me to receive some courtesy trousers which he had taken from the burliest member of his team! What a pro!

Literally nothing was too much trouble in those days, and everything was taken care of. If you wanted a cheese sandwich in your room at 3 am, you simply called the PR man and they would contact room service for you and sort it out. If you had a problem with your room, such as a broken shower, unattractive wallpaper or a lot of sick on the carpet, you simply phoned the PR's room and they would attend to this issue. Even when an alleged motoring journalist had an alleged dead hooker in his room on what was alleged to be the launch of a medium-sized family car from an alleged French car company, the PR was alleged to have made the problem allegedly go away. They must have done a good job in this case because the culprit has long since retired and moved to Whitehaven in Cumbria to open a B&B with his wife and the police in Cannes still haven't caught up with him as far as I know.

Of course, on any launch in those days, there was always driving to be done, if there was time. This too led to some high jinks and I dread to think how many speeding tickets and parking fines various PRs had to make 'disappear'. Mind you, if they could get a dead whore out of Nigel's room, paying off the local cops for a few tickets was probably a walk in the park. I remember once returning to a hotel near Nantes on the launch of a small Japanese car and running very late as I had been driving alone and I had become very lost in those pre-sat nav days. As a result, I was wringing out this little car for all it was worth and travelling at quite some speed along French lanes when suddenly and, quite by chance, I realised I was about to pass the gates to the Chateau where we were staying. With barely any reduction in speed, I yanked on the wheel and screeched into the long driveway, which swept downhill towards the front of the magnificent building. As I did, I could see the lights twinkling on the terrace to the right of the main entrance and realised that it was my esteemed colleagues already enjoying a drink in the warm twilight air. Accordingly, I hammered the throttle once more and the tiny car whirred up to maximum speed as we tore down the long gravel driveway towards the building. Unfortunately, at some point between the gate and the chateau, it started to become clear that I had lost something which, to be more specific, was control of the car. As such, I left the driveway itself and went onto the grass, this causing the car to enter both a spin and then a small gazebo, neither of which did much to counter the downhill momentum, which continued through four full rotations until progress was mercifully halted by a low stone wall right in front of the very terrace I was attempting to reach. Having come to a halt, I simply stepped from the car, walked up the steps at the side of the terrace and, in one smooth move, accepted a glass of wine from the ever-professional PR man. Truly, I felt like James Bond, but in one of those scenes where he's bleeding profusely from the head and then pukes onto a French journalist!

On another occasion in the middle eighties, I recall returning to the hotel after the driving exercise and casually mentioning to the PR that there had been a slight prang as I pulled into the car park that evening. "Don't worry", he quipped. "We build one of these things every 45 seconds!" Quick as a flash, I shot back, "Well your production chaps are going to have another four-and-a-half minutes' work tomorrow!" which he found terribly amusing, although, in fairness, this was before he saw what had actually happened.

Naturally, I can't think back to these glorious days when car launches were good without mentioning the 'gifts', commonly referred to as 'blags'. These were typically a little memento of the launch, such as a Swiss watch, leather jacket or case of vintage wine, and it is far too easy for cynics to say that these are 'bribes' or 'sweeteners', which is absolutely not the case. First of all, I do not need an Omega Seamaster or consignment of Petrus to tell me how excellent a car is. Secondly, these gifts are actually an example of how well-mannered car companies are, or were, as they're really a way of saying thank you for taking the time out of your busy schedule to join us on the private jet or at the five-star hotel or on the yacht, and that seems perfectly reasonable to me. Plus, as I mentioned earlier, the journalist gets a pleasant reminder of a certain launch every time he uses his video recorder or 21-year-old Balvenie, especially if the car manufacturer has taken the time to put their logo on it. Some did, though some respected that this might be inconvenient if, for whatever reason, the journalist later decided to sell the gift to someone else. The generosity of the car industry in the good old days was delightful, and it wasn't just gifts to take home because there were certain instances of other paid-for 'presents' turning up in journalists' rooms, and these ones had legs, arms, tits etc.! I should stress that I did not take advantage of such offers back when I was happily married, but they were certainly welcome when my marriage turned out to be less happy and then non-existent.

If you're a layman, you might still be puzzled as to why car companies used to spend so much time and effort on car launches. Indeed, I remember once telling someone in the pub about where I had been recently, what I had experienced and how this explained why I was wearing an orthopaedic shoe, and I was shocked when his response was, "So that's why bloody cars are so chuffin' expensive!" I found this response absurd, especially as I never had a go at him for having two weeks in Malta every summer just after putting his beer prices up again. Anyway, the reasoning behind car launches in those days was simple. First of all, the use of private aviation or first-class travel was purely a time-saving measure because PR knew that motoring journalists were busy and that, if they were required to be away for six days to test a new car, every minute counted, whether it be with the speed of private check-in or, at the very least, the use of a priority lane at a major airport. But why, you may ask, does a car launch need to be overseas in some sunnier clime? Well, quite simply, ask yourself this; how is a professional journalist supposed to assess how a new model looks if it is grey and drizzling? They can't, which is why they need sunshine. Also, photographers claim they need it for their shots. Finally, why the use of five-star hotels and the very finest restaurants? Again, this was perfectly easy to explain and, once again, it came down to convenience. If everyone was billeted in some basic B&B, can you imagine what would happen if a journalist suddenly woke up in the middle of the night and wanted a beef sandwich or realised that he'd left his eczema cream in the UK and needed someone to get him some more? The proprietor wouldn't know what to do when the PR came to him with these requests and, most likely, they would go unfulfilled, whereas a high quality hotel is used to making guests as comfortable as possible, whatever their needs, and that meant the journalist could relax in total comfort, which meant they were more able to concentrate on the car they were reviewing.

So, you see, it was all perfectly logical when you wanted it to be. Unfortunately, this was not necessarily the view held by the dullards and nitwits in the accounts departments of some car companies and, over the years, I have seen signs of a decline in the length and quality of car launches, plus I went back to the regional press and got bumped down to the UK launch rotations for many models. This careless and selfish reduction in standards at far too many car concerns is one reason why I was actually quite glad to get bumped off the international launch roster once I went back to a regional paper as, in many ways, the UK is more convenient and still has plenty of nice hotels in it, more on which anon. Nonetheless, I'm always glad that I was on the overseas launch scene in those heady days of the 1980s when things were done properly. They really don't launch 'em like that any more, as I shall explain later.

# 7. HOW TO WRITE ABOUT CARS

If you think that motoring journalism is simply about driving around in other people's cars and then going back to the hotel for a wine and a big dinner and maybe a dump and then some more wine and perhaps a whisky or two, I'm afraid you are not completely correct. Motoring journalism is also about writing. This may come as a surprise to some of you, but trust me, you simply cannot get a piece of computer software to write car reviews for you and, frankly, that whole project was a total waste of money. As a motoring writer, the simple fact is you must spill words onto the page like so much Châteauneuf-du-Pape onto the marketing director of Renault.

So, you might ask, how do you write about cars? Well, at the risk of stating the obvious, you use words. But car writing uses some very specific words and part of your job is not only to use them but also to know what they mean, e.g. camshaft, bell housing, suspension knuckle, underfold. In this way, car writing is more complicated and technical than, say, Jane Austen, who never used any of these words, as far as I'm aware. Perhaps she should have done and her books would have been less terrible. Anyway, the point is that motoring journalism is more complicated than normal writing by dint of it being about sophisticated pieces of engineering and, while you don't need to know every last piece of minutiae about double wishbones, anti-roll springs or variable phase outlets because you can copy that stuff from the press pack, it's definitely an advantage to understand the basic principles of how a car works or, indeed, after you've driven it into a low wall, why it doesn't. That means familiarising yourself with things like the four basics of internal combustion, that is to say, suck, squeeze, bang, blow, which rather reminds me of a hooker I encountered in Houston, Texas, though some of the other things she did are not currently part of how car engines work, e.g. piss stuff.

Assuming you are at least slightly familiar with the basics of cars and know the names of the things they have, such as doors, wheels, cams and boot flap, then we move on to a very important part of motoring journalism; describing and assessing those things using the written word. It can be dangerous to over-analyse the process of writing because, in many ways, it should flow out of you, like free-form jazz. However, you must also be aware that simply writing down the first thing that pops into your head can be bloody awful, also like free-form jazz. For that reason, writing needs thought and time and, sometimes, a drop of writing lubricant. This is particularly important for car writing because this craft demands two important elements. First of all, it needs to be informative. That is to say, it needs to give the reader who might be interested in buying this car some functional pieces of information. How much does it cost? How fast does it go? Are the seats comfortable, supportive and relatively stain resistant? Which airbags suddenly deploy in the event of a high-speed kerb strike? Does the Bluetooth phone make it easy to contact the relevant authorities/Honda's press office? These are the kind of practical, basic pieces of fact that you should include, and woe betide you if you don't because Peter Sladd of Wood Lane in Harrogate will write you another bloody letter asking why you didn't mention the engine size again. It was a 1.4 litre, Peter, now piss off.

The other side of motoring writing is quite different. You see, when writing about a car, a motoring journalist has to acknowledge that, while some of your readers want facts (those who are thinking of buying this model, plus Peter Sladd who bloody well isn't because he's had the same Mazda 323 for years, the pedantic tit), the vast majority of the audience is not on the cusp of a purchase and simply wishes to be entertained. Therefore, you have two pillars of motoring writing; informing and entertaining, and also trying to hit the word limit. On this last point, newspapers and magazines employ people called sub-editors whose job it is to make the words fit exactly on the page and, while they can usually cut out a few bits of a submission that are too long, they get very huffy about articles that are too short to take up the space on the page and will ring you up and then get into an argument with you and will take exception to being told to "sodding well sort it out" and will then run your test of the Jaguar X-type 2.2D with a gap at the bottom and the words "Roy Lanchester couldn't be bothered" underneath. Since I'm on this subject, that's another lesson that should be heeded when writing about cars; sub-editors have a surprising amount of power and, wherever possible, you should try not to have a series of heated arguments with them, even if they are a nit-picking idiot called Wesley who brings in his lunch from home in a Tupperware box and has a terrible beard like a child molester. Obviously, this advice doesn't apply in the online world where there doesn't appear to be any sub-editors, since children who can't write seem to think they don't need them.

Back to my point about informing and entertaining. The inform part is largely a matter of getting the right numbers out of the press bumf or, if that is not available, a matter of writing some placeholder copy and hoping that Wesley doesn't have one of his stupid beardy tantrums on the phone with you and later writes "to discover the horsepower output of this car, please contact Roy directly", followed by your home phone number. Although, on the plus side, this will be all the ammunition you need to get the pasty shit a massive bollocking from the editor.

Anyway, the 'entertain' part is arguably more important in car writing, yet is also a less exact science. What it boils down to is trying to use more interesting ways of talking about a car, and that comes from the use of words and the way in which you put those words in order, i.e. sentences.

Let me give you an example with the two sentences below:

– Sentence 1: "This car has excellent roadholding, though the engine is rather lacking in power."
– Sentence 2: "This car grips like a vice and corners as if it's on rails, but the motor couldn't pull my ex-wife off another lesbo."

Which sentence did you find more appealing? That's right, it was sentence 2. Why? Because it uses metaphor, simile and colourful language to paint an entertaining picture of what the car is like, to the delight of the reader. This is what motoring journalism should be like, unless you work for something boring and factual like Car Choice magazine, which, thankfully, I don't, since they turned down my application in the late 1980s.

Many people think it was another outspoken Yorkshireman, one J. Clarkson of Rotherham, who invented the metaphor in relation to cars, but nothing could be further from the truth. Yours truly was spicing up his copy with analogies and getting needlessly accused of racism back when Mr Clarkson was still in nappies. Assuming he wore nappies into his twenties, which, for legal reasons, I must point out that he probably did not. His jean trousers were plainly too tight for that. Any road, as we say in Yorkshire, I have long believed that a well-chosen comparison and a lively word composition are vital in car writing to offset talk of wheelbases and compression ratios and other things that, these days, you can cut and paste from the online press kit. By way of example, I offer this excerpt of my Rover 800 road test from 1986:

At long last, the Austin Rover Group has come up with a replacement for the long-running Rover SD1 beloved of bank managers, police officers and other irritants. It's called the 800 Series and is a joint venture with Honda, the Brits supplying their own styling and 2-litre engine, while the Japs have led the way on the chassis design and donated a 2.5-litre V6 engine for top models. There will also be a Honda version of this car, called the Legend, though trying to tempt British executives into a Japanese-badged car is surely a kamikaze mission.

First impressions of the 800 Series are impressive, with scalpel-sharp styling completed by neat details such as the integrated door handles on the driver's side. I presume the passenger side to be the same, though I didn't walk around the car to check. Out on the open road in the 820i variant, one finds that the home-grown four-cylinder engine pulls like a train, though is also prone to grumbling like an awful stepfather at higher engine speeds. In general, this new twin-cam, 16-valve motor could have the measure over equivalent power plants in rivals such as the excellent Ford Granada. The Jap-made V6 in the 825i variant is a little less excellent, however, with barely enough low-down grunt to pull over a crippled child, and this motor demands to be rowed along with the gear lever as a result. Nonetheless, both models can easily achieve the kind of speeds that could see you leave the road and have to walk back to the hotel, but the V6 feels a little lacking in balls. Perhaps this is seen as a bonus amongst the Nips, but it may not find favour with busy British executives. Privately, ARG bosses admit that more torque would not go amiss but note that their Honda colleagues do not see this, though they did not agree with your correspondent's suggestion that this was down to their having narrower eyes. Back on the road, one finds the chassis of both 800 Series models, designed by Honda and refined by Austin Rover, are excellent, with razor-sharp handling and limpet-like grip, plus a ride that is generally as smooth as silk on all but the most rutted of roads. Inside the car, one finds an attractive dashboard array with all controls logically arranged and, in general, falling easily to hand. The seats provide more than adequate comfort for busy bottoms and the rear pew, though not class leading, is certainly spacious enough for an average-sized captain of industry. His golf clubs will fit comfortably in the boot too, thanks to a low sill that aids easy loading. Overall, Austin Rover have done a first-class job of creating a new executive model for the mid-eighties, its efforts hampered only by some lazy work by their partners in Japan. The 800 Series will cost from around £10,500 for the forthcoming 820e up to approximately £18,500 for the top-of-the-range Sterling model. This car represents a Daley Thompson-sized leap over the ageing SD1 and is sure to give the Ford Granada, Vauxhall Carlton and various foreign rivals a bloody nose in the executive car park.

This test may be over 30 years old, but it could have been run last week, if anyone in this day and age still wanted a first drive road test of the Rover 800. You cannot fail to notice that the use of language is still fresh and relevant, and this is something I have always believed you should aspire to in motoring journalism, if you are doing any. Frankly, there is no excuse for boring writing, and if your editor accuses you of such a thing, just claim to be very tired. The advent of computers has, of course, made it even easier to write interesting reviews since, with a mere right click of the mouse, the writer can access an in-built thesaurus, which saves the author from having to unearth the trusty paper version of such a tome, once the most faithful confederate of any scribe.

At this point, you might believe that the job of a motoring journalist is easy. You think you know about the basics of cars, you think you can write a road test where you remember to include the price and you're confident you won't get another shirty note from the PR man at Nissan just because you accidentally said their new Qashqai has 28bhp. You might even think that you can wrap all this up into entertaining, amusing, enjoyable, compelling, entertaining copy. Perhaps you're even thinking that, one day, you could have my job. Well, you can't. First of all, the job is still mine and will be until the day I die, and don't try suggesting that day will come "in the next two weeks" because I get enough of that nonsense from my GP and local taxi company. Secondly, it's not that simple because there are other factors to consider, such as tone, and I don't mean the chap who works in the bookies on Tadcaster Street, although he too is surprisingly hard.

Tone is sometimes referred to as the 'house style' and, unlike 'house wine', is not the kind of thing to be avoided whenever someone else is paying. Look at it this way, the style you would adopt when writing for one publication is not necessarily the style that would be acceptable when covering the very same subject matter for another outlet. It is very important to understand this and to adapt your writing to the newspaper or magazine you are working for. By way of example, here are two pieces that I wrote back in 1998 and which I recently unearthed on a floppy disc (for younger readers, this being what, these days, you would call 'the cloud'). One of these reports was for The Harrogate Herald and one for the then-new North Yorkshire youth magazine NYORKS, for which I had recently secured the motoring page gig under the pseudonym Rick Lanch. Normally, I wouldn't have been interested in such a job, aimed as it was at young idiots, but the editor was a pal of mine at the Lodge (this being just before I was asked to leave the Freemasons following a situation with a furious chief superintendent) and they'd got a load of start-up investment which, in those days, was a clear invitation to jack up your freelance rate. Both of the pieces below concern the same car, the mk2 Renault Clio, but you should be able to spot a subtle difference in tone to suit the publications' respective audiences.

What happens, homers? Rick Lanch coming in you with all the updates on a wheels so hot and cool it's mild! I'm chattering of course about the new Clio from those Froggy hitmakers at Renault. This is all-new Clio, fresh for '98, taking it to the max for increased refinement. Outside-wise, it's well fit. Get inside her and it's wicked with all controls in your face. Those funsters all fall to hand on easy street. This baby got drive too, 'cos she doesn't just look like a Parisian supermodel, she goes like one too. Performance is well wicked and handling is on the rails. The new Clio is fresh and direct in your local Renault bitch right now! Check it out!

Displaying the tardiness for which they are famed, it has taken the French a full eight years to replace the original Renault Clio with this brand new mk2 version, primed to enter battle in the fiercely fought supermini sector. Of course, given the Frogs' general track record, war-wise, it's a miracle they didn't ask the British to help out as usual, though, as far as I am aware, they did not and Renault representatives on the launch event seemed to resent this line of questioning. Therefore, we must assume that this new machine is as French as smelling of garlic and then being very rude when someone points this out. One certainly can't fault the styling, which is a neat evolution of the previous model and presumably designed to look good even when covered in dents, having been driven for a few weeks in its homeland. They may be bad at parking, but our Gallic neighbours are certainly skilled when it comes to making a bonny baby car and it looks good from all the angles I stood at, which were generally at the front. Note also that, while the French can't be trusted with things such as infrastructure and other men's wives, they can usually be relied upon to make a sassy chassis and, in this department, the new Clio does not disappoint, offering a ride as pillowy as a Parisian madam's bosom and roadholding that grips like moules-frites. Add in standard engines that tug like a traction engine and you've got a package that's sure to give the Fiesta, Nova, Polo et al. a bloody nose. Don't just take my word for it, however. Head down to Stan Bingley Renault in Harrogate right now to check out the all-new mk2 Clio for yourself!

In case you were wondering, the first sample was for NYORKS and the second for The Harrogate Herald. Even to the untrained eye, you may have spotted some differences between the two works, notably that the first example was shorter. This is because the editor who commissioned this piece had rightly identified that young people are stupid and have no attention span. That said, it was around this time that management at The Harrogate Herald had decided that the elderly and those who only wanted news from Harrogate and the surrounding area couldn't be bothered to read lots of words either, hence my road tests were generally cut down to the 300–400-word mark, to be surrounded by much shorter and punchier news stories, known in the trade as 'nibs' and known in my house as "a pain in the arse to put together". You may also notice that the NYORKS report employed a 'trendy' style of slang and was generally less informative, whereas The Harrogate Herald story relied less on gimmicks and gave much greater depth. I should add that both pieces re-produced here were my original submissions and they were not printed like this for a variety of reasons, one being that NYORKS folded three issues in and before they could run my Clio test, and another being that the bloody subs desk got their fingers into my Herald words once again while some weedy snitch told the editor that I was trying to plug the local Renault garage within my copy, even though it was none of their business who was or wasn't helping me out with a small gambling debt.

While we're talking about writing, I should also add a note about deadlines. These are the dates by which a newspaper or magazine will expect your words to be delivered and woe betide you if you miss this date, as you'll probably get a whinging call from some mouse-faced cretin like Wesley demanding to know where your work is, at which point claim to have a migraine, even if you don't suffer from such things, which I don't, as they're only for women. In my experience, deadlines are all made up anyway, apart from the ones on daily newspapers, which are very real, as is the warning note on your personnel file if you keep ignoring them. In other words, deadlines are like the best before dates on food; they can be ignored, but to do so may cause you to shit yourself.

In summary, writing about cars might appear easy, but that is not the case. In fact, if you are considering a career in motoring journalism, I would strongly advise against it, as most newcomers to this business arrive with bright-eyed eagerness and a strong work ethic, neither of which is doing anyone any favours. In my experience, it is experience that gets you where you need to be in car journalism and where I need to be is in car journalism, so do not attempt to steal my work, if you please. However, beyond that, there is also the technical issue of actually being able to write, and many people wrongly assume that, just because they like cars, they can write about them, whereas this is simply not the case. In fact, many people haven't got the first clue how to write about cars and yet still cling on to prestigious newspaper columns nonetheless. To sum up, never assume that you can write about cars because not everybody can, although, luckily, I am not one of those!

# 8. THE FIRST TIME

I have always been blessed with a reasonable memory, something my GP has often described as "remarkable, considering". For example, I can remember where I was and what I was doing when I heard about events as varied as the first election of Margaret Thatcher (in a garden centre), the invasion of the Falkland Islands (fist fight with a hotelier), the fall of the Berlin Wall (trying to get sick out of a travel kettle) and the death of Sir Bruce Forsyth (birthing a turd). However, my memory isn't perfect and that's why I've always made an effort to write things down, a trick drilled into me by my first editor, Cyril Crest, after he reminded me that court reporting relied on accuracy and not simply describing someone as 'swarthy'. These notes have come in very handy over the years for filling in some of the blanks, as it were. After all, they say if you can remember the late eighties in car journalism, you probably weren't on the Peugeot 405 launch in Tangiers! Well, I was and it's one of the reasons for the heavy scarring on my left thigh. Thankfully, however, I have always prided myself on keeping extensive notes and doing so in extensive notebooks, all of which I keep on a shelf in my house, which is extensive. The only gaps in my records being those notebooks lost to the fires and the ones still held as evidence by constabularies in North Yorkshire, South Yorkshire and Berkshire, and also Portugal. In addition to these minor gaps, there are those from the period in the early nineties when I was on some strong painkillers and attempted to invent my own shorthand. The leather-bound tomb from the Mazda Xedos 6 launch at Wellsham Hall in Gloucestershire is largely unintelligible as a result, though someone has clearly carved 'DUNGHOLE' onto the back. It could have been me, I simply don't know as I was rendered insensible by my physician's failure to warn me of what would happen if the medication was combined with a '78 Bordeaux. His negligence later resulted in significant damage to a vintage armoire.

Anyway, thanks to my note-taking, I am able to look back on past events with an accuracy that was so sadly lacking when manoeuvring between two pieces of furniture at Wellsham Hall. I have always considered this a bonus, as it's fair to say that, in motoring journalism, you get to do, see and fall into a great many things. However, there are certain moments for which notes are not required, as they will always live on in your mind, unless you befall the fate of my Auntie Eunice, who became convinced her own brother was a man from the council coming to steal her taps, though I'm certain she put on a lot of this just because she found her family tiresome. Anyway, my point is that, in life, you never forget certain events, or at least the way the medics explained them to you afterwards. Speaking personally, I can still remember my first accident in a car (shat my pants in a Fiat Mirafiori), my first road accident in a car (Fiat Mirafiori, moments after the above), my first trip on a private jet (Ford Granada facelift event, Sardinia, terrible turbulence) and my first bill for breaking the lavatory door on a private jet (see above).

Also in the category of things I will not forget (unless I do an 'Auntie Eunice' and start hiding all the teaspoons in a Quality Street tin) are my experiences with supercars. What is a supercar, you might ask? Well, opinions on this vary and the publisher has asked me to remove the definition I had borrowed from another book, so let's just say a supercar is very fast and often has the engine in the middle. They're also quite rare, which is why any drive in one is memorable, largely because it probably requires you to visit the manufacturer's factory, since they usually refuse to drop one to your house. However, in many ways, this only increases the mystique and the prospect of a decent lunch before/after/during your drive.

My first experience in a supercar was back in 1983 and the vehicle in question was the legendary Lotus Esprit Turbo. Prior to this, I had enjoyed no dealings with the Norfolk-based car maker, but with my new status as the motoring correspondent on one of Britain's leading newspapers, I felt it was important to telephone their press chap and remind him who I was. Sadly, when I first rang, I was informed that he did not work on Wednesdays and when I rang back the following day, it turned out he did not work on Thursdays either. Subsequent attempts to track him down were met with either no answer or an unhelpful one from someone with the kind of countryside accent that makes them sound like a simpleton. Younger readers must remember that, in those days, there was no email and all telephones were wired into the wall, making them much easier to ignore and/or trip over. Eventually, however, I was able to track down the elusive PR, a nervous chap called Bert Furstly, and introduce myself as a man who would like to test a Lotus. This was an interesting time for the small company because, on the one hand, their products had starred in not one but two James Bond films, while, on the other hand, their founder had recently decided to 'add lightness' to himself by being buried in a nearby churchyard (i.e. he had died). I decided to capitalise on the former by suggesting to the PR man that my readers might like to know what it was like to drive the car that 007 had used in a movie just two years ago. I should add that this was some years before I had the brilliant idea of testing all Lotus Esprits and Aston Martins by being photographed leaning on them wearing a dinner suit under the headline 'Shaken not stirred?' but I still thought the Bond angle was strong. Sadly, the PR man disagreed with some parts of my plan, specifically in the area of delivering a new Esprit Turbo to my London home for a week and instead suggested that I pay a visit to their factory in Hethel, near Norwich, the following month. Having established that lunch would be provided, I cautiously agreed.

I recall that I drove up to Norfolk that summer in the Vanden Plas version of the new-for-'83 Austin Maestro, having been unable to sample this version on the launch due to a spluttery bottom situation brought on by a bad sandwich. I seem to remember it was a generally excellent car, spoilt only by a terrible smelling interior, as I had inadvertently left some wet clothes in the boot for a couple of days and even removing them didn't seem to reduce the level of odour/condensation. Nonetheless, I arrived at Hethel in good spirits and was immediately met by someone who didn't know where Bert Furstly was or, indeed, what he did. After an hour or so, this was remedied by another rather simple-sounding woman who informed me that Furstly had gone missing but that he had asked her to take me out to the test track. Here, I was immediately struck, firstly by a reversing Ford Escort and secondly by a magnificent Esprit Turbo, resplendent in white with red stripes up the flanks and a small man inside it. This turned out to be one of their test drivers, who was on hand to "show you what she can do", the "she" in this case being the car, rather than the dim lady from the marketing office. I didn't catch the man's name as he appeared to be foreign, or perhaps Scottish, but he certainly kept to his word and really stretched the low-slung Lotus's legs on the old airfield they called a test track. This being my first experience of a supercar, I was rendered speechless and then queasy by its obvious performance and handling capabilities. The more pedantic among you may quibble here with the definition of the Esprit Turbo as a true supercar on account of its mere four-cylinder engine, but let me tell you that I had no such doubts when I took the wheel for myself, as this machine certainly had the looks, the power and the ability to make you lose control at 130mph and end up in a field of potatoes.

The elusive Mr Furstly later found this fact somewhat unamusing, though I repeatedly explained that it's very hard to engage in high performance driving when there is a certain amount of sick coming from your face onto the steering wheel, gear lever and passenger. The foreign test man was equally unamused at the time, although it was hard to make out the specifics of his complaint.

My other memory of that suddenly truncated day at Lotus is that, as I was leaving, I encountered a group of people crowded round another Esprit, one of whom I recognised as Lotus Formula 1 driver Nigel Mansell. There was no issue with this, as it was some years before the incident.

After my truncated time with the Esprit Turbo, my supercar experiences kept on coming during that heady decade we now refer to as the eighties. Another one I will never forget is the first time I stepped into a Lamborghini. The low driving position, the narrow windows, the unlabelled open-gate gear change, the distinctive high-pitched wail of the PR man as I reversed over him. It was an experience like no other, apart from the part about running over a PR, which I had already done twice before, three times if you count getting the chap from Ford again going forwards. I have always admired Lamborghini for their outrageous styling, V12 engines and wine, but when it comes to Italian supercar makers, there is one that truly stands out for mystique, glamour and famousness around the world. I'm talking, of course, about Ferrari, and I can still vividly remember my first encounter with this company and its products.

My first and only visit to their factory was in late September 1987, and came about after a lengthy conversation with their communications director, whose name I cannot spell. After much persuasion, it was agreed that I would visit their hometown of Maranello in order to drive the then-new 328 GTB. The flight would be paid for by my newspaper, but my hotel and meals would be taken care of by the Prancing Horse themselves. I would negotiate sundries such as cigarettes and new trousers as and when required, with the knowledge that I could probably put them through expenses at The Examiner. At the start of the allotted week, I flew from London to Bologna, where I was collected from the airport by a Ferrari employee in a Lancia Thema and driven at some speed to Maranello itself and my hotel, which was near the famous factory, although I didn't know this at the time. After checking in to this charming guest house, I made my way to the restaurant across the street, where I enjoyed a hearty lunch and a robust bottle of Chianti, which I followed with a strict instruction to send the bill to the hotel across the street for the attention of Ferrari. The proprietress was happy to do this, as far as I could work out. I then retired to my room for a short nap and awoke to find with surprise that it was dinner time, so back across the road I went to find the food just as excellent and the Barolo extremely quaffable. The following day, I took the opportunity for a walk to a different restaurant for lunch and then got down to business with a hearty ravioli, plus a bold Chianti back in the original eatery across the road at dinner time.

After three days, it occurred to me that I should ask about driving the car, so I arranged for the hotel to telephone the communications desk at Ferrari. Shortly afterwards, two factory representatives arrived at my lodgings and informed me that, yes, something would be arranged very shortly, but that first we should go for lunch, which we did. By the time lunch was complete, the working day was over and my hosts departed, leaving me to contemplate the next thing on the agenda, which was dinner. The following day, one of the communications representatives surprised me during lunch with news that, tomorrow, a car would be made available for testing purposes on the understanding that I did not drive it. This is ridiculous, I replied, for I am a professional motoring journalist for one of Great Britain's best-known newspapers. I did not come to Italy to spend a week eating pasta and drinking wine at someone else's expense, I continued, and I must insist on extending my stay until a car is available to drive. After the weekend, it was agreed that I could get behind the wheel of a car, on the understanding that I would not criticise it. I explained in no uncertain terms, and with some necessary references to Italy's performances in both wars, that this was utterly preposterous, after which there was a full and frank discussion about my hotel bill and some of the things charged to it, until it was eventually agreed that the keys to a Ferrari 328 GTB would be made available to me just as soon as the effects of lunch had worn off, by which time it was dinner and my drive was re-scheduled for the next day.

Unfortunately, the next day, it was explained to me over lunch that the car was not ready, as my visit was somewhat unexpected, having been planned just a couple of months ago. By way of apology, the communications representatives asked if I would like to visit the factory to look at some old racing cars, an invitation I happily accepted on the understanding that we went for dinner afterwards.

Twenty-four hours later, I was ready to go, but it turned out to be some kind of saints day and everywhere was closed except, mercifully, the restaurant across the street from the hotel, which was still serving, although the veal was off. It was particularly hot that day and, as a consequence, I started lunch with a bottle of white, before moving on to a bottle of red, a process I used to humourously refer to as 'pinking'!

Finally, the following day, we were ready to go, as long as the man responsible for maintaining the car said he was happy, which is something he couldn't do on account of having the day off. The day after, however, all the stars finally aligned, unlike the door on the Ferrari 328 GTB, which did not. It was explained that the car must be "perfect" and it was taken back into the workshop to be mended while I was taken back into the restaurant near the factory to be given some more pasta and a robust Barbaresco, after which driving was ruled out for a number of reasons, one of them being the imminent arrival of dinner time.

The next day dawned with some incredible news; the car was now ready and mine to take away (for no more than one hour). I thanked the communications men profusely and regretted that I had long since forgotten their names. Finally, it was my time to drive a Ferrari for the first time, and it was an experience that would live in the memory for many a year. The roar of the mighty V8 engine behind me, the clack of the hefty but delightful gear change, the weighty yet precise steering. Truly, this was a bright red dream machine and, even today, I can remember the experience of flying down the straights like a rocket, scything through the corners as if on rails and reversing into a low wall as if it wasn't there, although, in fact, it was there and the communications men saw me do it as, unfortunately, it was inside their factory. Fortunately, there were no hard feelings about this, at least on my part, and I left the premises in high spirits as well as a hurry, still giddy with excitement for the rest of the day, knowing for certain that it was a Thursday I would never forget.

To be honest, my skin was still tingling a little as I boarded my flight back to London the following Monday, although that might have been due to the bed linen at the Italian hotel, which had definitely aggravated my eczema. However, it was certainly also due to the experience of driving a true supercar on some of the roads upon which it had been conceived.

Though I had enjoyed my experiences with a Lotus and a Lamborghini prior to my delightful fortnight in Maranello, it was that Ferrari driving experience in the 328 GTB that taught me both what a supercar was all about and also what it cost to repair one. Fortunately, when the bill arrived at The Examiner offices, it was in Italian and I was able to sneak it through expenses as accommodation costs, (even though Ferrari had paid for those, minus the last 300 quid's worth of drinks).

Yes, my time in Maranello and, in particular, my time behind the wheel of a Ferrari was truly a moment in life I shan't forget, though it also became memorable because I got home and found that my wife was leaving me!

# 9. THE END OF AN ERA

My life in the central part of the 1980s had been a happy one. I was the respected motoring correspondent for one of Great Britain's most respected newspapers (notwithstanding some of the flack they got for their coverage of the Northern Ireland 'troubles', which personally I thought was the kind of tough love the pesky Paddies needed). I was held in high regard by the automotive press officers of this land and treated with the kind of reverence that only evaporates when you tell them you're going back to a regional outlet. Best of all, when I wasn't staying in fine hotels and driving some of the middle-eighties' most exciting and/or practical cars, I went home to a spacious rented flat in London's East Finchley to the woman I loved, that is to say, my wife Marie.

In many ways, my life in the period 1983–87 was very much like the second term of Mrs Thatcher's administration, which covered the same period, because, having seen off a foe (in her case, the Argies, in mine, my annoying first wife) and entered a period of successful consolidation, she/I was at the very height of her/my powers. Unfortunately, just like Mrs Thatcher, my halcyon period was brought to a horrible end and yours truly didn't even have to wait until 1990 to get stabbed in the back, as my Michael Heseltine was also someone with excellent hair who I thought I could trust, that being my own wife.

What I enjoyed about my marriage to Marie was how little she interfered in my business. I could be away for two weeks on back-to-back car launches, or just the single launch of the Peugeot 309, which really did go on for a while, and she would offer not a word of complaint. Plus, I would often return with a bag full of small hotel soaps and shampoos (unattended housekeeping trollies are a godsend for inexpensive gifts!), which I know she enjoyed greatly and were undoubtedly the reason why she always seemed glad when I went on another trip abroad. For my part, I never minded that she took a new job on the arts desk at The Examiner and was often out late of an evening reviewing some film, play or gallery because it meant I could go to the local pub as I pleased. On the same note, I never had any objection to her taking weekends away with female friends, which she did with increasing regularity. After all, it would have been highly hypocritical of me to spend five days on the mk2 Vauxhall Carlton launch in Grand Cayman and then make a fuss if Marie wanted to spend a long weekend in the Quantocks with an old gal pal from art college.

Ours was a harmonious relationship based on the main principle of a happy marriage, which is not seeing too much of each other. She had her job and her interests; I had my career and my duty as main bread winner to come home with the bacon, sometimes literally, and also, perhaps, a Talbot-branded radio-cassette player. When we did spend time in each other's company, I enjoyed, as I always had done, her impish sense of humour and dry wit, and my only real complaint was her reluctance to get stuck in, bedroom-wise. Overall, I thought life and wife were both in fine fettle, until that fateful day in October 1987, when I returned from a slightly extended trip to the Ferrari factory to find Marie waiting for me with what she described as "news". In this case, the headline would have read, "LANCHESTER'S WIFE A LEZZA" with a sub-head of "Top motoring hack's muff-diving missus to leave with immediate effect". I'm not sure if muff-diving needs a hyphen in it, but the subs could have decided that one. The main issue for me upon receipt of this news was not an argument with the pedantic tit desk about colloquialisms for homosexual lady people, but that my beloved wife, according to a source best described as "herself", had not been happy for some time, had packed up her things and was now leaving me on account of not fancying men.

Such was the speed with which this unexpected news was dispensed that I had no time to think of what to say before she stood up from the sofa where we both sat, pecked me once on the head with a soft kiss and then picked up her suitcase and left the flat. I didn't even have time to tell her that, in the absence of decent toiletries in my Italian hotel, I had bought her some fancy soap at the airport using my own money and not even asking for a receipt. It was too late. Quite unexpectedly, my marriage had been dashed on the rocks surrounding the Isle of Lesbos.

I don't mind telling you that I wept that evening. I wept and wept and opened the new bottle of Scotch I'd also bought at the airport, and then wept and wept some more. It was two full weeks before I heard from Marie again and, in that time, I was not at my best, as anyone on the BMW 3 Series facelift launch in

Munich would attest. At the time, I had not let on about the disastrous bomb that had gone off in my personal life and, when I found myself suddenly howling "NOOOO" and running from the room during the technical briefing, my journalistic colleagues must have assumed that I was sarcastically reacting to news that the turbo diesel derivative would not be coming to the UK.

When I heard from Marie again, it was a phone call to see if I was "okay" and then to ask if she could come by to get the rest of her things. I implored her not to be hasty, but there was a cold determination in her voice and that strong will I had always admired was now working against me. I knew that she was set on making this break permanent and nothing I could do or say would stop her leaving my life forever, taking her remaining belongings and, though perhaps she never realised it, my heart as well. Sure enough, a few days later, I attended the Daihatsu Fourtrak refresh event near Peterborough and, when I got back, her things were gone.

In my attempts to make her stay, I had rashly stated that she could have the Austin Metro I had bought for her (at a substantial press discount) some three years previous, little guessing that, one day, that class-competitive British small car would betray me by allowing her to clear her stuff into its surprisingly roomy interior, perhaps taking advantage of the once-innovative 60/40 split folding rear seat that had impressed me back on my first press launch in 1980. However, there was a small silver lining to all this because the Austin Rover PR man was still shirty with me about a recently borrowed Metro press car that had been returned with what appeared to be the wheels and well-used tyres from my wife's car on it, and I was now able to blame this entirely on Marie, while adding that, in all honesty, I did not know where she or her car on its fresh new tyres had gone. This, however, was of very little compensation for the Marie-sized hole left in my life. There was no pleasure in attending even the most luxurious of car launches knowing that I would not be coming back to her, while going to the pub alone lost some of its appeal without the knowledge that there was someone at home who wouldn't nag me about it when I got in.

I had long since cottoned on to the concept of 'working at home' and rarely attended The Examiner offices, save to turn in expenses and collect my post once every two weeks. However, since Marie was still working there, I realised this was my chance to speak to her and to see if there was any chance of reversing her decision to both leave me and become a lesbian. Accordingly, one Thursday, I drove into town in a Peugeot 405 SRi press car and went up to the main office in the hope of catching her off guard. It was to no avail. Her desk was clear, her typewriter covered, her personal effects nowhere to be seen on the bare wooden surface. Marie Anne Lanchester, née Sugg, had left the building. The sour-faced old cow who did secretarial work for the arts desk refused to tell me where she had gone, and was clearly still smarting after an incident the previous year when I'd suggested we had similar sized moustaches, but I managed to find out from Rob Gosley on the sports desk that she'd quit even before breaking up our marriage and had gone freelance with a regular gig for the arts pages of The Sunday Sentinel. He added that he believed she'd recently spent some time back in Ely in Cambridgeshire, which is where she was from. So that was it, she was gone from my home and gone from my place of work, leaving a hole in my life as gaping as if they'd taken the cathedral from Ely itself (i.e. massive, because the cathedral is out of all proportion to the rest of the town, or 'city', as they insist on saying, the idiots).

In retrospect, I think it's fair to say that I did not cope with the end of my second marriage and my wife's descent into lesbianism as well as I thought at the time. While going through various boxes of papers during the making of this book, I came across a typed report on the Volkswagen Passat mk3, which I would have written in March 1988 or thereabouts, and it gives a clue as to my mood in the months following Marie's departure. I reproduce some of it here:

This is Volkswagen's new entrant in the hotly contested medium segment, taking on the Ford Sierra and Vauxhall Cavalier, though, unlike either of those big sellers, it lacks the option of a hatchback body style, and this may cause UK buyers to wonder why VW has bothered. Indeed, why does anyone bother? One can put in effort over many years only to be rewarded with a slap round the face or a stab in the back and only then do you question why you bothered at all. Or perhaps, at this point, you begin to wonder, was it your fault? You might think you're making an effort but it's all too easy to take someone for granted, little guessing that you are pushing them into making decisions that will have a lasting effect on both your lives and, yes, maybe that's some excuse, but it's really not excusable to be such a two-faced bitch and to treat someone so badly in this way with no hint of a warning about what's to come, I just can't even begin to understand it, and how can you claim, how on earth can you claim to love someone and then just pack up all that you own and desert them. Speaking of which, the Passat is certainly notable for a very commodious boot.

If you re-read this extract, you may notice a subtle but present undercurrent of something that goes beyond a mere review of a new mid-sized Volkswagen and gives a hint that all was not entirely cheery with yours truly around this time. The reason I still have this report is that it was never filed to The Examiner, as my previous week's submission, though billed as an in-depth look at the all-new Fiat Tipo, was, in fact, just Marie's name typed repeatedly onto seven sheets of A4. This did not go down well at the paper, which, as of early '87, was being edited by former deputy editor and noisy Cockney oaf Kevin Leather following the retirement of esteemed editor Lionel Purchase. The regime alteration had already put my relationship with the office on a different footing, pre what I came to refer to as Mariegate. Leather and I had always enjoyed a reasonable relationship. After all, it was he who was partly responsible for hiring me, but I felt power had changed him and, when we spoke, which was rarely, there was a new frost in the air, such that it no longer seemed affectionate when he called me a "fucking prick". Hence, when I hit my lowest ebb and started turning in some less-than-ideal copy, Leather wasted no time in telling me to "sit it out for a bit". To my annoyance, I later discovered that, in my enforced absence, he had given motoring duties on the paper to freelance writer and cravat-wearing twat Egan Coates, whom I knew and disliked from the launch circuit. Coates boasted the kind of laid-back suaveness that is only possible if you grew up with money and particularly irritated me with his casual references to his "Lotus" which I happened to know was only a 1970 Europa. Even more irritation was to come when I realised that Kevin Leather's suggestion to sit it out for "a bit" actually meant "permanently", a fact that was made clear by a letter from The Examiner personnel department which arrived in April 1988.

All was not looking well for Roy Lanchester at this time. No wife, no job and, to cap it all, my press car booking for the then-new Toyota Carina was cancelled without warning, no doubt down to the turncoat Coates gleefully passing on news of my decision to be released from my position. Determined not to be beaten by the downturn in my personal and professional circumstances, I busied myself with trips to various local pubs and this occupied a few months until the enforced closing of various bar tabs, plus the high cost of paying a private detective to find out where Marie had gone, forced me into a less-than-ideal situation when it came to liquidity, in both the money and the other sense. But for the rest of a case of Châteauneuf-du-Pape I had left over from a Renault launch, I really was at rock bottom and, just when I thought that things couldn't get any worse, I received a phone call from my theoretical stepfather telling me that my mother was ill.

I should explain that, in about 1981, my mother had married again, this time to a pointless man called Peter Pigeon. Marie once pointed out that, technically, this made my surname Lanchester-Pigeon, adding that this sounded like a particularly crappy aircraft from the inter-war years. As I've said, I always loved her dry wit. Suffice to say, I did not change my name and nor did I have much to do with this man, who was both short and a geography teacher, these also being the two aspects about him that I found most annoying. He and my mother had met at some hand-wringing church group for people who couldn't hack their booze, mother having been taken there by her friend Diane Forrest after the gin situation got a little too much. Pigeon was in after getting busted buying whisky miniatures from an off-licence during a morning free period at school. My mother once told me that he was everything my father wasn't and at least one aspect of that had turned out to be true, because he had, thus far, proven himself to be quite good at sticking around, much to my displeasure. Now here he was in his stupid geographical voice telephoning my flat to tell me about my mother's liver, once so full of gin, now so full of cancer.

So I had no wife and no job and now I learnt that my mother back in North Yorkshire was dying. I realised my life was over in London; it was time to head home to the north, especially as I'd run out of money to pay the rent. There was nothing left for me in the south now except for a black hole where my life used to be, and a gambling debt of the kind that was best to run away from. With a heavy heart, I managed to call in what I thought would be one last favour from Ford, packed up all of my things and hit the M1, where, I must add, the then-current 'aero' shape Transit press demonstrator proved itself to be the consummate cruiser, even heavily laden, and boasted car-like comfort levels, as well as impressive mpg figures on the run back to Harrogate. The London chapter of my life was now closed and I was, once again, living with my mother in my hometown, just as I had 10 years previously, although now she was in and out of hospital and, therefore, unable to cook my tea most nights. Also, it was not the family home in the former sense, as mother had sold the old place when she married Pigeon and the pair of them had bought a 1950s detached house on the outskirts of town. I didn't realise it at the time, but this would, one day, become my actual home, but that was all to come.

My mother, Lillian Lanchester, passed away in June or July of 1988. I'd stopped keeping notes during this time as there seemed little point. Anyway, it was definitely the summer. Her funeral was surprisingly well attended, although I was disappointed that my father didn't show his face, as it was some years since we had spoken. I imagine he was busy or didn't get the news until it was too late. With the cremation out of the way, we moved swiftly on to cheerier things, like the reading of the will and, here, I was in for a nice surprise, as it turned out my dear old mum, perhaps imagining that she would outlive the irksome Pigeon who was some eight years her senior, had left me the house! This seemed only fair since she had basically paid for it, Pigeon apparently having no money when they married on account of an earlier divorce and then blowing what was left on whisky miniatures. Why the stupid idiot didn't buy large bottles and decant the contents into smaller containers I do not know; the cost saving would have been significant over time. At this low point in my life, discovering I had a four-bedroom house on the outskirts of Harrogate was the small boost I needed and I wasted no time in making the place my own, i.e. by telling Peter Pigeon to get out. If this sounds harsh, I should add that he had a daughter nearby with whom he could move in, and if that didn't work out, I'm sure he had keys to the school and could bed down there for a bit.

The house inheritance was a great boon and another was just around the corner when I took a trip to Leeds in search of radiator spares and decided to call in to the Your Yorkshire offices, just for old times' sake. In those days, it was still possible to walk straight into the editorial offices, a shoddy security arrangement that was later changed after one of the news desk got assaulted by an irate fishmonger, so I strolled into my old stamping ground to find almost no one I recognised, save for sports reporter "Basically" Bryan Hobbs (so-called because he used to say "basically" far too much, long before it became fashionable) and noisy art desk irritant Ross Cockling, who loudly shouted, "Bloody 'ell, it's the return of the prodigal twat." I didn't take offence as this is the natural reaction in Yorkshire towards anyone who has had the temerity to move to London and then come back again, even for a weekend. After this jocular start, Cockling and I had a quick chat, during which he asked if I was back to take the "motoring job" at The Harrogate Herald. "Maybe", I replied enigmatically, while making a mental note to find out what the bloody hell he was talking about.

Using my well-honed journalism skills, I quickly rang the offices of the Herald and asked if they were looking for a motoring correspondent. Using the power of what I imagine was some sort of small, desk-mounted switchboard system of the kind that was being phased in around this time, the receptionist put me through to the deputy editor, who confirmed that they were. Immediately, I told him who I was (Roy Lanchester) and what I wanted to do (get a job on his newspaper). The deputy editor later turned out to be a genial chap called Langley Bostrum but, for now, he was simply a softly spoken man on the other end of the telephone making encouraging noises about my credentials, many of them formed into words such as "experienced", "calibre" and "useful", none of which I had heard in relation to my career for some time.

To add a little context here, while my former employer, The Harrogate Post, had decided to become a slender weekly freesheet with a view to going out of business in 1993, which it did, its great rival, The Harrogate Herald, had just received a significant boost, having been bought by the massive Anglian And Associated Regionals Group (AAARG), who had invested to make the Herald the premier paper in Harrogate and the surrounding towns. As part of this push to be less crap, budget had been allocated for, amongst other things, a proper motoring section, this being seen as a great way of getting in more ads from people with proper budgets, such as car makers, car dealers and, to a lesser extent, the people who sold roof racks and crap like that.

A week later, I met with Bostrum and Herald editor Max Hampson, both of whom were, I could tell, deeply impressed with my background and cheerfully willing to overlook the awful mess I had made in reception due to several things out of my control, one of them being a plastic cup of soup. Suffice to say, the job was a shoe-in, which, ironically, was what also happened to the broken display stand in their reception area, and, later the very same day, Langley Bostrum telephoned to say that they would like to take me on as a freelancer with a monthly retainer to be their new motoring correspondent! I wasted no time in getting this information out to the wider world (of the car industry) and, within the month, I was on the Suzuki Vitara launch near Peebles. Yes, I had lost a wife and a life and a mum, but on the plus side, your correspondent was back in the motoring game!

# 10. ON THE BOX

After the sad loss of my job/wife and the slightly less inconvenient loss of my mum, I soon got my life back on track with my new motoring page in The Harrogate Herald and my new (inherited) house, both of which benefitted from not having Peter Pigeon in them. It certainly felt good to be a motoring journalist again, I thought to myself, as I quaffed a glass of light lunchtime wine on the Renault 19 launch in early '89.

Of course, writing about cars is all well and good, but, at some point in a car journalist's life, they're sure to turn their thoughts to a darker, dirtier, more expensive media mistress. Not Janet from the Phastpix picture agency in Stockport, although someone once told me the same broadly applied; I am, of course, talking about television. The haunted lantern, the goggle box, Nicholas bloody Witchell's house. Talking about cars on the old telly screen has become a popular route to fame and fortune for many a car journalist, not least household names such as James "Slow" May, Richard "Captain Hamster" Hammond and, of course, Jeremy Clarkson. They might make it look simple, but then they have an army of off-screen writers, producers, researchers, hair stylists, clothes operatives and bottom wipers to do all the hard parts for them. Unlike a bafflingly large number of the great unwashed, I have absolutely zero interest in these overgrown schoolboys and their shenanigans, save to say that I wish them all the best and hope that they enjoy the ill-gotten gains of their buffoonery, such as Ferrari 458 Stradales, Porsche 911 GT3s, Volkswagen Golf GTIs and ample houses in Hammersmith, Herefordshire and Chipping Norton plus a large flat in London's Holland Park, where he spends the week.

I should add that I met Clarkson once, many years ago on a car launch when he was a fledgling presenter on the first iteration of Top Gear and I was very much at the top of the game in the regional newspaper motoring review business, with over two award nominations and almost no pending legal actions. "I've seen your efforts on the telly, Clarkson", I began, clapping him warmly on where his arm would have been if he hadn't moved it at that precise second, causing me to slap him awkwardly on the rib cage. "I must say it's nice to see a fellow Yorkshireman ont box", I continued. "Even if tha dunt sound lak it and is talking reet posh and that." I was hamming up the accent by now, in case you hadn't noticed. "Course, appen the difference between me and thee is that I still live in Yorkshire", I concluded with a wry smile. "Exactly", quipped the man himself. "And that's one of the reasons I left." With that, he walked off to look at a wall chart about gearbox input shafts. I've always remembered that encounter and I'm sure Clarkson will recall a fellow Yorkshireman on the VW Vento event in 1992 and, indeed, the events that led up to my sudden removal from the venue. I imagine it probably put him off Crème de Menthe for a while!

The thing about Jezza is that everyone imagines he invented politically incorrect banter about cars on the television. Well, they're wrong, because I believe a certain person got there first and that person was yours truly. Yes, I too have been on the other side of the camera in my career. (By which I mean I have been a TV presenter, not that I was once a cameraman. To be clear, the side of the camera that I was on was the lens side, i.e. the part that captures the images, rather than the viewfinder side occupied by a man wearing a fleece, though I have nothing against fleeces and am wearing one with Peugeot Rallye Sport stitched onto it as I write.) In fact, my television career began in 1984 when, as the motoring correspondent for The Examiner, I was invited onto the Sunday evening current affairs show The Week In View, which was made at the London Weekend Television studios and transmitted live on ITV stations across the land. This was an unusually highbrow show by the council house standards of "Idiot TeleVision" as I used to call it, and I was honoured to be invited to appear as a pundit to discuss news that Nissan had signed a deal to build a UK factory. Given that I had never appeared on the moron's lantern before, I felt that I acquitted myself extremely well and certainly did not deserve to be collared after transmission by an unpleasant producer woman bandying around words like "sweaty" and "racist". To be clear, I believe to this day that doing an accent, whether Japanese, French or Jamaican, is not racist, though I know some people think that using your hands to make your eyes a different shape is a grey area. Anyway, although I was never asked back, I felt I did well and was quite the natural on The Week In View, something I was able to confirm, having recorded the live transmission at home on the video recorder I had just picked up on the mk2 Fiesta launch. Things then went surprisingly quiet on the TV front for me until 1986, when I was on the Rover 800 Series launch mentioned earlier in this book and encountered a BBC news crew who were covering the launch of this important new British car (and, knowing the Bolshevik Broadcasting Corporation, bemoaning the fact that trade union troublemaker Red Robbo had been sacked). After dinner one evening, I suggested to their producer that I had some thoughts about the car and was willing to dispense them into their camera, which, after another glass of broadcasting juice, I did with aplomb. Annoyingly, however, my sterling (no pun intended!) contribution was not used in the finished news story, perhaps because the producer had wrongly believed that I was "slurring" and that my affectionate tribute to Austin Rover's colleagues at Honda was "unnecessary". Why on earth do TV people have such a problem with the Japanese accent, I wonder? I should add that I was not cut out entirely from the BBC news report as, if you watch back the bit where they're interviewing Roger Blessing from The Mercury, you can just about see me in the background trying to get free from the curtains.

That was it for Lanchester on television until 1989 when, thriving in my new role at The Herald, I was at the poorly catered UK launch for the facelifted Nissan Micra when I encountered a TV producer by the name of Brian Clave, who told me firstly that he wasn't the waiter and couldn't get me another glass even if I said "chop chop" and, secondly, that he was looking for new talent for an experimental motoring programme to be pitched into the exciting new world of satellite broadcasting. "I have a real problem with people who talk about cars on TV", Clave told me once I had secured another refreshment. "They're all so boring and serious. I want someone with opinions", he concluded. "I have opinions, you fat shit", I replied, bravely. What you have to remember is that, up until that point, no one on television had expressed an opinion, but I was about to change all that. Clave was clearly impressed with what he saw and heard, even though this later included me being sick behind a velvet chair, and, a week later, I was in the offices of Sirrius TV in Manchester for a chat with Clave and his colleague, Martin Can't remember his surname. Their pitch was simple; we want to make a one-off taster programme to showcase our ideas in the hope that they will be taken up for a full series by fledgling satellite broadcaster Orbital UK. In the TV world, this type of show is called a 'pilot', not to be confused with the kind of pompous man who tells you to get off his aeroplane. The two men wanted their programme to have lots of 'attitude' and 'freshness', and I was happy to make clear that I was the man for the role, since people often commented on my attitude, if not my freshness. I was delighted when they eventually agreed with me and even more delighted when they suggested we continue discussions over lunch in a local pub.

The following week, we set a plan to film an item with yours truly at the helm and, with a bit of cajoling and an agreement not to submit any more dry cleaning receipts for what happened on the AX five-door launch, the press chap from Citroën agreed to invite myself and a film crew of four on the UK first drive event for the new XM executive car. With the event secured, Clave and I faxed scripts back and forth as we refined the words I would say and fleshed out the list of words I couldn't. In this respect, I found it rather wearing how often 'the powers that be' seemed to intervene with the express intention of neutering some of the 'attitude' for which I had been hired and which Clave and Still can't remember his surname were so enthusiastic. In the end, compromises were reached and, while the PC police reluctantly agreed that I could, for example, say, "And thanks to a 2-litre 16-valve engine, it can go like a Parisian hooker on heat", they were most insistent that I subdue lines such as, "The sleek plastic bumpers will help reduce repair costs in the event that your lesbo ex-wife reverses into something while trying to leave you, the fucking bitch."

Soon afterwards, filming was upon us and we met the night before our shoot at Shellingham Manor near Nottingham, from where the launch would be based and where I was able to show these TV types how a car event worked. We began with the usual rather tedious technical presentation, during which I made some of my customary amusing asides about the French performances in Wars 1 and 2, whilst the PR boss made his customary attempts to hiss, "would you mind saving this for later" at me. Then, it was time for dinner, at which I urged my new television friends to "get stuck in" and they replied with disappointingly lily-livered responses such as "but I don't really drink" and "the man already told you, there are literally no more prawns in the building". I should also note that many of my colleagues in the journalism game were clearly fascinated by my move into TV, not to say obviously jealous, as they sidled over with a range of quips, such as "I hope you've got a wide-angle lens" and "let's hope it's not smell-ovision". Envy is a terrible thing, but I should add that I had the last laugh, since at least two of these jocular fellows are now dead.

The next morning, we arose at a time that was apparently normal to these television types with their fancy talk of "schedules" and "time" and "of course it wasn't a joke, why the hell didn't you set an alarm?" The director had already secured a silver XM and positioned it at the rear of the Manor, overlooking the attractive gardens, and it was here that he asked I deliver my first piece to camera, in which I established that "This is Citroën's new entry in the hotly contested executive market and which the company is hoping will make an interesting alternative to established rivals such as the Vauxhall Carlton and Rover 800, with advanced suspension, hatchback practicality and a ride that's more pillowy than a French handmaid's knockers."

With this delivered over several takes, I became aware that all was not well in my guttural region and pondered the wisdom of popping inside for a precautionary turd. Alas, before I could express this to the crew, the rather bossy director ordered that we "saddle up" and get on the road to record some of my thoughts from behind the wheel. With a cameraman sitting next to me poking his sizeable equipment into my face and the director behind him in the back seat, off we went and I did my best to speak my thoughts into the dark void of the lens, though my most immediate thought was that I shouldn't have had so much seafood last night. After 45 minutes of this activity, the director announced that he had "more than enough" and that, though he probably wouldn't use the part where I described the dashboard as "dog shit" and then did a sicky burp, he did have enough material to "cobble something together".

For our next scene, the camera was set up overlooking a quiet lay-by on a country road with a pleasant vista behind and I was asked to pull into the shot, stop, get out and deliver my thoughts on what executive car buyers are hoping for, although this differed from what I was hoping for, which was "a toilet". Poised further up the road, I awaited the signal from the director, accelerated forward, pulled up to the agreed point, removed my seatbelt, opened the door, stepped from the car, closed the door behind me and then voided myself in a manner that was most certainly not in any recent draft of the script. I made this unfortunate development immediately clear to the crew and the director announced that he had "definitely had enough". With that, the crew got back into their Sierra estate filming car and departed with the promise that they would "let me know" about the pilot episode. All that was left for me to do was drive the XM gingerly back to Shellingham Manor, inform the PR man that there had been a re-run of the AX five-door incident and then head to the bar after a quick cleanup.

A new type of car TV had been invented that day, in which the presenter really said what he thought and didn't really think what he was saying, though, of course, I didn't realise it at the time and nor did anyone else. A few weeks later, Brian Clave rang to say that the pilot episode had not been well received and no future series would be forthcoming, but that he would happily send me a VHS tape of our endeavours, now branded as 'Road Burn'. I received a package from Manchester a week later, happily coinciding with the receipt of a new video player from the Daihatsu Applause launch at Dalston Hoo, as the unit from the mk2 Fiesta event had become broken after ingesting some things that weren't VHS cassettes. Upon playing the episode, I was disappointed to discover that the show was full of hyperactive editing, strange camera angles, gimmicky graphics and silly effects in which presenters were falsely made to sound as if stammering, such as in the very titles of the show, which repeated the phrase 'Ro...ro...road B...b...burn!', all in the manner of 'youth' TV that had become popular at the time. My disappointment was compounded when I discovered that other presenters received the bulk of screen time and that my own efforts, perhaps by dint of being too ahead of their time, had been reduced to one ad-libbed line which was used as a heavily treated 'jingle' between sequences, presumably for 'punky' effect.

It was clear by now that television was not for me. It takes a long time to make, it lacks the subtlety and expressiveness of the written word and it's full of stifling 'politically correct' types who don't want you to say "leather like a dead dog's ballbag" into the camera. Nonetheless, I feel proud of my own far-sighted venture into this TV world, knowing that, in effect, my outspoken efforts invented Jeremy Clarkson, as well as his sidekicks The Captain and Slow Hamster. With this in mind, I sometimes put on that old VHS of Road Burn, if only to see and hear my younger self saying "Jesus Christ, sorry Nick I've just sh...sh...[record scratch effect]... shat myself."

# 11. ALL CAR COMPANIES GREAT AND SMALL

In all my years as a car journalist, which, to be absolutely clear, are not over yet, I have seen a great many car companies come and go. What I have learned, however, is that one cannot discount some of the new boys when they appear, as they may lead to something big, just as equally they may go bankrupt almost immediately, leading to an awkward encounter with the failed company owner in Hilton Park services when he tries to claim you were to blame, just because you said his stupid sports car was deeply uncomfortable for anyone with large thighs and also a deathtrap. However, for every Cizeta or MG Rover, there is a Pagani or a Marcos (before they went out of business). That's why it pays to keep a close eye on any new entrant to the merry carousel of the car world. It can be all too easy to stick to the established, larger car-making concerns with their ample press fleets, comprehensive insurance and accommodating hospitality budgets, but that would be to miss out on some innovative newcomer who may have come up with a fine piece of engineering and might offer you a pub lunch once you've driven it.

While going through some old notebooks for this book, I came across two interesting examples of 'left-field' car companies that I noticed long before anyone else, both of which I encountered in 1990. One was a 'one-man band', the other a much larger concern. At the time, I decided both were worthy of attention and, in many ways, I was proven correct, notwithstanding that both don't exist any more. But that's not really the point, as I shall now explain.

My experience with the smaller of these car companies started when I was contacted by a well-spoken gentleman called Henry Leominster-Fisher, who wished to tell me about his "exciting new sports car" (his words) and he was so full of affable optimism, as people often are when they've come from money, that I agreed to pay him a visit, even though normally I "couldn't be bothered" (my words). On this occasion, I made an exception because a) his premises weren't too far from where I lived and b) I was trying to stay 'off the radar' as far as the Herald was concerned, at least until the fuss had died down about who had broken the office fax machine and how. Also, in the plus column, Leominster-Fisher promised that his car was "really something special" and also that there was a "smashing pub" near his workshop at which we could "discuss things further". I was willing to take him at his word on both counts and made an appointment to visit him the following week.

Eight days later, and within two hours of the allotted time, I arrived at LF Motor Cars' premises, a prefabricated shed-style construction in Ainderby Steeple, which is generally near Northallerton. Here, I was greeted by the ebullient Mr Leominster-Fisher, whose attire made it quite clear how posh he was, and his business partner Mike something-or-other, whose trousers were much less upmarket. The latter was the 'chief engineer' for the project which they had christened the LF1, while Mr Fortesque-Lemons was the 'brains' behind the styling and all other aspects of the vehicle, including, I presumed, the money to make it. They made an unlikely pair, with the engineer being rather quiet and withdrawn, while the other chap was loudly well-spoken in that excessively confident way that makes normal people uneasy around the upper classes. Anyway, this unlikely pair led me through to their workshop and, with a great flourish, revealed the car to me by whipping away a sheet, something that never works because it always gets caught on the door mirrors. Once the two men had unhooked the sheet, I was free to gaze upon their machine and I must admit that it was not unattractive in a sort of deliberately old-fashioned way, rather like Mr Posho-Posho's jacket and, indeed, house, the ample rear of which was visible from the premises. If you crashed a Morgan Plus 4 into a 1950s MG TF and then plonked the wreckage onto some Ford Sierra parts, you'd have had a close impression of this car, although its creators got needlessly sniffy when I suggested this. Nonetheless, they were happy enough to answer my various questions about on-sale date, performance and when might be considered lunchtime around these parts. "Tell you what", boomed Mr Frosted-Glass at a rather strident volume, "I'll take you for a spin in her, we'll swap over and then pop to the pub for a bite to eat." This was excellent news and, as the car was only a two-seater, it meant Mr Engineer couldn't come along, which suited me perfectly, since I'd already heard enough about Ford gearboxes. With that, Frobisher-Fartshead eased the car out of the workshop while I thanked Engineering Man for his enlightening monologue on the tunability of the Pinto motor and let him go back to whatever it was he did in there when the public school chap wasn't around. Reading a Haynes manual to a state of arousal no doubt, although I remember noticing they had an actual titty calendar over the workbench, as was perfectly reasonable in those days before the PC ninnies started whining to the EU about such things.

After waving goodbye to the boffin, I lowered myself into the LF1's snug passenger seat and off we went with Loudly-Inheritance at the wheel, parping along the country lanes at quite a lick until, with a pop and a hiss, a coolant hose came off the engine. "Not a problem!" barked my host after some inspection of the engine bay, and, with that, he removed his tie, used it as a makeshift oven glove with which to squeeze the pipe back into place and then marched up to the lone house outside which we had expired. When the door was answered, he used a honking tone of intimidating self-assurance much seen amongst the upper orders to command the occupant to give us a jug of water to top up the coolant and we were soon on our way again. "Obviously, that won't happen with customer cars!" he shouted as we continued our journey before pulling into a gateway some four or five miles later so that I could take the large, wood-rimmed wheel. I must confess that my first impressions of the LF1 were not bad. Yes, the old-fashioned looking bodywork was at odds with the use of Ford instruments, column stalks and seats, and the ride was as lumpy as my first wife's custard and thighs, but it cornered as if on rails and the 2-litre Sierra engine pulled like a train, relieved as it was of having to move around an actual Sierra.

In general, I was quite impressed as we finally pulled into the pub car park and I accidentally reversed into a low wall. "Obviously, that won't happen with customer cars!" I quipped, which Mr Floppy-Cocknobbins did not seem to find amusing. Nonetheless, we entered the pub where they seemed to know him, which was fortunate because if anyone talked at that volume and in that accent in one of my locals, he'd probably get his face smashed in. He then bought me a pint and a sandwich and another pint and took great delight in running me through his business plan in somewhat needless detail, since I had left my notebook in his workshop. In fact, such was this plummy chap's enthusiasm for speaking about "recapturing the spirit" of something or other that I had to insist on another pint and a follow-up before, mercifully, the pub was closing for the afternoon, at which point I realised the quick Scotch at the end had probably pushed me over the old drinking limit for being allowed to drive and I was forced to ask Mr Wobbly-Poshknob if I could come back to his house for a well-earned snooze. He agreed (albeit very reluctantly, which struck me as poor form since he plainly had plenty of bedrooms) and we took the FL1 back to whence we had come, before I was shown into his house and introduced to his wife, both of which were attractively proportioned. Mrs Friggme-Sideways showed me to a spare room and I was able to sleep off an intense lunch before making my excuses, apologising for what happened to the vase and heading home in my Rover 400 Series press car. So what became of LF Motor Cars and its well-to-do owner? Well, suffice to say that, when their car finally went on sale, it sold only a handful of examples, which was nothing to do with my review in a regional newspaper, despite what they might have tried to claim to the contrary. Unfortunately, setting up a car company, even a small and stupid one, is a pricey business and I later heard that Mr Farty-Parp-Parp was, as his wife tried to claim about the bedspread in their spare room, "ruined".

This, of course, is the issue with these newcomer car concerns and, while the motoring journalist might believe he is driving the next big thing, there's every chance he's actually motoring around in someone's forthcoming bankruptcy. Nonetheless, you can never ignore these dreamers, especially if their wife keeps ringing your office to demand payment for a new "throw", whatever the hell one of those might be.

However, it's not just the small and obscure car makers that I have kept an eye on during my career (to date). During the 1980s, it became clear to me that there was a troubling uprising happening in the British car market, and this threat came from cheaply priced, low quality cars from the Communist Bloc. Personally, I thought anyone buying such a thing might as well move to Russia if they liked it so much. Indeed, had I been in charge, I would have arrested them upon leaving the showroom for their treacherous desire to fund Boris' lethal nuclear ambitions towards the bastions of democracy and the free market. Mrs Thatcher certainly had their number, and I did too, as I steadfastly refused to test drive any of these awful Commie cars during the 1980s. Besides, their importers were small and rarely had the budget to organise an event worth attending, with precious little hope of an overnight hotel, never mind a decent dinner. They'd probably serve you a potato and make you sleep in a gulag, knowing that lot! Nonetheless, these terrible cars did find an audience, largely made up of pale-faced loony lefties with donkey jackets and bad posture who lived in their delusional socialist utopias such as Sheffield. I must admit, I was secretly intrigued to sample one of their cars so I could say how awful it was, but my zero-Commie policy could not be waived.

However, in 1989, the people of Poland finally saw sense and threw off the shackles of Communism under the direction of that docker chap with the decent moustache and his Solidarity Party, which still sounded a bit lefty to me but can't have been as bad as the mad Trots who'd been running the show from Moscow. Finally, it seemed as if Poland was ready to look west and embrace the wonders of capitalism, such as central heating and not queuing for bread. It struck me that buying a Polish car would now be socially acceptable and, bang on cue, in 1990, the country's leading car maker, FSO, announced that it was to re-start importation of cars to the sunlit uplands of Great Britain. I received this news through their newly appointed UK PR operation, which was a man called Gryff who was from the Polish city of Swansea. It was only later that I discovered he was Welsh as, on the phone, a lot of these foreign accents sound the same. Anyway, this man filled me in on FSO's plans and then invited me on a 'fact-finding' trip to Poland itself, where I could see the FSO factory for myself and have a drive in their new Caro model, which would be arriving in Britain very shortly.

Keen to show my support for the plucky Poles and their new-found plan to embrace the free market for medium-sized hatchbacks, I said yes as soon as I had established that this was an all-expenses trip, which it was. I was also delighted to discover that this entire junket was just for me and no other journalists, which I considered a huge bonus, especially as I was trying to steer clear of Phil Snell from The Woking Mercury, who was STILL carping on about how much fondue cheese got onto his wife. The UK PR Welshman would not be joining us either, which was a relief, since I still couldn't understand much of what he was saying, and, instead, I would fly straight to Warsaw, where I would be met by some local operatives on the ground. This was the perfect arrangement, since there would be nobody to make stilted conversation with on the plane and, when the drinks trolley arrived, nobody on board to tell you to "slow down", except the cabin crew and co-pilot.

So it was that in mid-1990 I caught my flight to Warsaw, looking forward to filing the exclusive, hard-hitting test of this re-born former Commie car which I had already promised my editor. I should point out that, in those days, Poland was quite an unknown for British people, as this was long before half their country decided to come and live in our country, taking all our jobs, sucking up our welfare benefits and fixing most of the damage to our bathrooms for a fairly reasonable price. Thus, I had little idea of what to expect as my worryingly Communist Polish Airlines jet touched down in Warsaw and I walked out of whatever their word is for 'arrivals' to be met by a man from FSO called Peter, although it almost certainly wasn't spelt like that. My first surprise, and relief, was that he spoke remarkably good English, probably better than his PR compatriot back in the UK, who had a terrible habit of mixing 'was' and 'were' in a most irritating manner. Using this amazingly fluent ability in proper language, Peter (Peiter?) invited me to follow him outside to the car park where a colleague was waiting and I was delighted to discover she was a rather attractive girl called Sylvia, though, again, it probably wasn't spelt properly. To my relief, she too appeared to have a decent grasp of God's own tongue and she used this to inform me that, as per Polish tradition, they would now welcome their guest with a shot of vodka each. Accordingly, she turned to the car behind her, which appeared to be an FSO, although I didn't look too closely, and, from the boot, produced a bottle and three small glasses. These were brimmed, my hosts gave some sort of exclamation, which I presume meant "cheers", since it was unlikely that they both sneezed at the same time, and then the cold, clear liquid was downed and then the car was entered and a road joined, and the FSO factory driven towards. During this journey, Sywllia in the back seat offered forth another cool, crisp shot of vodka and then another, although not for Peter (Pietr?), since he was driving what, by now, I had definitely identified as an FSO, since it said so on the dashboard. Shortly, we arrived at our destination, which was the FSO headquarters and assembly plant, although the sign seemed to need about 37 words and far too many consonants to make this point. I must confess that, although the streets we had driven down seemed rather grey, dirty and depressing, it was not such an alien urban landscape, especially if you were familiar with Doncaster. Likewise, the factory itself was not the blackened ex-Commie slave ship I had expected but largely resembled a dirty, 1960s factory of the type we had plenty of at home. One could have easily mistaken it for the Austin Rover plant at Longbridge, especially as, during the past few decades, both were full of filthy Marxists! Not here at FSO, though, for they were looking to a bright, capitalist future and, as we entered the reception area of the factory, I was keen to hear more about some of the things Peter (Peatre?) and Silvwa had mentioned on our journey, chief among them being lunch. Sure enough, I was led upstairs to the 'senior ranking dining room' which, I was informed, was once quite a controversial place, though, these days, it seemed quite nicely carpeted. It was a decent sized room containing three large round tables and, since we were the only people in there, I took a seat at my leisure and allowed Silvlia to bring me the first of several 'traditional' Polish luncheon items, this one being another glass of vodka. Thereafter, there was some soup with an egg in it, some more vodka, some meat and a cabbage item of some kind, a little more vodka, a type of cake, a shot of vodka and then an opportunity to fall down a short flight of stairs. With that completed, we headed to the factory itself for a tour of the facilities which, Peter (Petor?) informed me, would comprise of the press shop, the body assembly facility, the final assembly hall and the quality control area. Unfortunately, there was one item omitted from his itinerary, which was the 'getting run over by a forklift' section, and this was almost immediately inside the first building we entered. The damage to my person was, thankfully, minimal, though my trousers fared a little worse and, as I pointed out to my hosts, they really ought to write 'keep to the walkways' in English as well as Polish in future. Anyway, after this unfortunate incident, it was agreed that we should cut short the factory tour and head back to the main building, where I could sit down for a cigarette and maybe a bit more vodka. I was installed in a comfortable lounge area with an excellent view of a car park and given 30 minutes to relax, smoke and enjoy a drink before Sellvia very kindly brought to me both the chief

engineer of the Caro hatchback and also another
bottle of vodka. Unfortunately, this engineer chap,
whose name I'm not even going to attempt to spell,
didn't speak much English at all, but Peter/Peeteer
did the translating, Cillvia did the pouring and, all-in-
all, it was a most enlightening conversation that made
me wish, in some ways, that I was still able to think
straight.

By the time we were done, it was time for
Peter/Peatr to drive me to my hotel for the night,
where I was informed that we would also dine this
evening, in the company of another unspellable man
who was something to do with exports. I was
pleasantly surprised by my room, which was simple
but comfortable and, to my surprise, contained a TV,
which must have been a relatively recent addition,
since I think they were banned under the Commies,
as was hot water. No such concerns today thanks to
the shipyard chap and his chums and, after a sleep
and a shit, I was able to enjoy a fairly warm shower
before putting on my other trousers and heading
down to the dining room for what turned out to be a
very convivial dinner with a man whose name
sounded like Robert but probably wasn't. He was the
exports manager for FSO and he told me they had
high hopes for the UK market in the 1990s, while I
explained that I had high hopes that he would ask for
another bottle of vodka to be brought over, as indeed
he did. I was truly impressed by my Polish hosts, in
particular by their ambition, by their enthusiasm and
by the way they got me up to bed without waking me.
There are few UK PRs who would do that!

The next day, the lovely Swyllya met me in the
hotel for breakfast. "I suppose you have vodka with
breakfast?!" I jested. "If you would like, Roy!", she

replied in a way which suggested I probably should and, once that was done, we drove back to the FSO plant, where I was introduced to another man whose name was mostly Z sounds and who was something to do with design. He took me into his studio, where I suggested we have some of the vodka I'd brought from the hotel and he suggested that this was okay, as long as I agreed to stop leaning on the wall behind me which, despite appearances, was not actually a wall. After that, I realised that, between breakfast and a brief chat with the styling man, it was now almost lunchtime, which was to be taken in a management canteen in the company of the factory manager, some hot eggs and another bottle of vodka. I was certainly impressed with the hospitality and by some things he told me via Peter/Pitr about output which he claimed was the best in Eastern Europe, though I'm sure he knew I was unable/unlikely to check this.

After lunch, there was just time to visit the quality control area, where Saliva insisted that British customers were particularly concerned about quality, value and one other thing that I didn't write down. Then, it was back to the hotel to get my things and check that the mattress had dried, a quick vodka downstairs to celebrate a most agreeable trip, then into the car to be driven to the airport for my evening flight back to the UK.

Upon arriving back in Britain, I got into the taxi booked by the FSO PR Taff and was gently dozing on the M1 when I suddenly realised that, after my two days with the Poles, I had completely forgotten to drive the car. This was a bloody inconvenience and no mistake, especially as I had made a point of telling my editor that I was bravely heading behind where the Iron Curtain used to be and intended to devote my entire page to lifting the lid on the Poles' progress in the car-making world.

After speaking to PR the next day, it became clear that there were no demonstrator cars in the UK, as the first imports had yet to arrive and I couldn't very well go all the way back to Poland, especially after the robust discussion I had enjoyed with one of their passport control goons on the way out. There was nothing for it but to give the impression that I had driven the car without actually claiming to have done so, formulating my impressions from my time in the passenger seat of the FSO that took us around Warsaw, although I couldn't really remember much about that thanks to the class-leading amount of vodka on board. Undeterred, I padded out the copy with some stuff about the factory and how impressive it was, and all was well, as long as you weren't concentrating too hard.

So, what became of FSO? Well, I'm sorry to say that they went from being an up-and-coming Polish car maker to being a non-existent Polish car maker because their stuff turned out to be crap. However, I learned a valuable lesson from my trip to Poland, which was that a motoring journalist should always try to drive a car before writing about it, if possible.

As for newcomer car companies, I believe that it always pays dividends to keep an eye on their progress and show an interest in their wares because you never know what you might get out of it. Just bear in mind that the odds are they'll keel over at some point whereas I am still working, rather proving that a certain failed car company owner's wife was talking out of her plummy arse!

# 12. CELEBRITY

One of the surprising aspects of being in the motoring journalism trade is that you can find yourself brushing shoulders with celebrities. Sometimes literally, as Judith Chalmers discovered shortly before she became instrumental in my removal from the Goodwood Revival. Over the years in this line of work, I have met many celebs, from Nick Knowles to Tony Hadley and from Linda Barker to Linda Barker again at another event a few months later. I have even become something of a celebrity myself, but more on that anon. I found Knowles, Hadley and Barker to be perfectly pleasant (Barker a little less so the second time, as she was clearly still smarting over the damage to her jacket), but most of the so-called celebs I have encountered have been little more than jumped up and self-important, only mingling in the car world for whatever freebies they can scrounge before promptly disappearing back to their ivory towers, leaving people who have a right to be there for professional reasons – i.e. journalists and, to a lesser extent, photographers – to explain away the damage to the curtains, which the venue refuses to believe was the fault of Paul Hollywood.

These 'stars' (in inverted commas) might seem nice and friendly on television but let me tell you that, in real life, most of them are not nearly as pleasant or, indeed, as tall. For every seemingly decent one, there's at least another troublemaker. Or, to put it another way, for every Sir Jackie Stewart, there is an Angela Rippon. Or, to put it in yet another way, for every chance to meet a hero of your youth, there is someone squawking about a "final warning" before the police are called.

Most of these alleged 'talents' (also in inverted commas) I would not cross the street to meet, especially if they're only going to hide behind a van and then cross back to the side I just came from while shouting "I don't want to talk to you, Roy", mentioning no names (Quentin Willson). But I bring up Sir Jackie Stewart because he is the exception to anything I might say about celebrities in general, or, indeed, the particular things I might say about Nigel Mansell, had the publisher not asked me to remove them. I have long admired Sir Stewart, right back to his early days when he was simply Sir Jackie and had always hoped that, one day, I would get to meet him in person. I don't know what it is about the man that I have always liked but I suppose what has always appealed is his combination of no-nonsense talking and air of fiscal prudence.

You can, therefore, imagine my delight when, in September 1991, I learnt that my old PR pal Kenny Heron had managed to secure the services of the legendary Scotchman to promote a product he was representing. I remember the phone call in which Kenny imparted this news and, more specifically, his response to my enquiry as to what Sir Jackie was like. The answer was swift, simple and did nothing to diminish my respect for the man; "punctual". During the course of this telephone call, I made it very clear to Kenny that he owed me £10 from a promotional trip to Bruges in which the hosting tyre company failed to provide enough refreshments and, latterly, napkins. However, I also made it clear that I would forget all about at least half of this debt if he could introduce me to Sir Jackie at some point soon.

It struck me that the diminutive wheelman and I might have much in common, since I too am of Scottish descent and I too once owned a brightly coloured tartan cap, even though two people on separate occasions said it made me look like "a tit". I had also heard many stories from his past that I wanted to ask him about, such as whether it was true that he was personally responsible for some of the well-sited control placement on vehicles such as the mk3 Escort, in which everything fell so easily to hand.

With this in mind, you can imagine my delight just a few weeks later when Heron rang to invite me to the legendary Brands Hatch circuit in Kent for an event to promote the new product for which Sir Jackie Stewart had been signed up, with the assurance that the man himself would be there! The product in question was a type of clasp that enabled an inertia reel seatbelt to be applied at the correct tension and was, therefore, just the sort of practical, safety-minded product you would expect Sir Jackie Stewart to be paid to endorse. Of course, this was not the sort of gizmo I would normally bother with unless the event was closer to where I live and there was the prospect of a room for the night plus dinner, but this was different because it was a chance to meet one of the few celebrities I truly admired. That's why there was absolutely no stopping me from attending this far-away event, after getting Kenny to agree to provide me with a room and at least two of the seatbelt gadgets to take away. All that was left was the small matter of how to get there. I knew that, for many years, Sir Jackie had been a Ford man, working diligently with the company to improve their excellent products with his unique Scottish experience. I, therefore, thought it only right and proper that I should telephone the Ford Motor Company and insist that they loaned me a well-equipped example of their Sierra model for the journey to Kent and a week before and after. The day prior to my trip, and mindful of Lord Jackie's famous attention to detail, I even went to the trouble of washing the Sierra, vacuuming the grass clippings from the boot and making a reasonable job of concealing the damage that had occurred to the wheel arch. With that done, I set off in good time the following day, as I was heading south and didn't want to get caught in rush-hour traffic on the M25 or, as I humourously called it, "the fucking M25". Accordingly, I arrived at a modest hotel not far from Brands Hatch by late afternoon and, after an hour or so for ablutions, I enjoyed a light dinner on the premises before heading out for a couple of drinks in a local pub and then one more in three additional pubs and then a Chinese. After that, it was back to my lodgings for a good night's sleep before the chance to be in the same room as none other than John Young Stewart. That's right, his real name is John, for using 'Jackie' as a nickname for John is one of those Scottish traditions, like being a tramp in England or pretending to enjoy bagpipes.

I rose the following morning in high spirits, showered, shaved, used the lavatory, showered again and then dressed, failing to notice that a listless late-summer bee had chosen to make its overnight home within the trousers I had left carefully upon the floor of my room. Clearly, it was a surprise to this stripy bastard to find itself suddenly within an enclosed space, just as it was an enormous surprise to me when the spiteful shit decided to deliver its poisonous dagger directly into the nearest piece of my flesh, that being a small sliver of scrotum betwixt thigh and underpant hem. With a great roar, I literally tore away my trousers as a searing agony consumed my nether regions, sending me flailing about the room like a crazed dervish, shattering the dresser mirror with my right hand and howling for the sanctity of my ravaged ballbag. Such was the ferocity of my anguished cries and the sound of breaking glass that, within moments, the proprietress of the hotel arrived at my door enquiring as to my well being and she seemed a little startled when I wrenched open the door and informed her that she must immediately look at my ballbag. To my great annoyance, she chose not to assist in the removal of the searing lance that was currently inflicting great agony upon my bollock sack but, instead, fled down the hallway and, by the time the police arrived, my eyes had stopped watering such that I had been able to pluck the lethal bee spike out for myself. Though still in immense pain, I was at least able to explain to the officers that, contrary to the landlady's high-pitched claims, I was not a profusely sweating, blood-sodden pervert; I was, in fact, a profusely sweating, blood-sodden journalist who was going to be late for an appointment with the legendary Sir Jackie Stewart.

In order to reach this historic meeting, my first challenge was to operate the controls of a medium-sector hatchback with only one good hand and a plum hammock that had swollen to the size of a grotesque novelty stress toy. My second challenge was gaining access to the Brands Hatch site itself, just 10 minutes drive from my hotel. Arriving at the main gate and announcing as best I could through ongoing spears of pain that I was "here to see Jackie Stewart" did not have the desired effect, as the surly and unhelpful security man took exception to the blood-soaked toilet paper wrapped around my right hand and then, upon asking me to step from my vehicle, the unconventional appearance of my unzipped trousers. It was the merciful intervention of Kenny Heron that saved this situation from becoming as ugly and swollen as my clanger carrier, as he had received word that there was a "large man" at the gate growling "it's my balls" at security. Never had I been happier to see Heron than at that moment. "Bloody hell Roy, look at the state of your trousers", he chuckled as he approached. "This is worse than Vienna." Nonetheless, he escorted me towards the Brands Hatch hospitality area where today's seatbelt symposium/Jackie Stewart meet 'n' greet would take place, permitting me to explain what had happened as best I could between hot and cold flushes and waves of nausea.

Upon arrival at the conference area, Heron was kind enough to find for me some replacement trousers, rather too small and of a tracksuit style, but superior to my own pair in the sense that they weren't torn through the crotch and covered in blood. Also, their soft fabric seemed to apply a little less pressure to my horribly distended jewel pouch and so, having squeezed into the courtesy trousers and mopped as much of the sweat from my face as I could, I re-applied fresh bog roll to my lacerated hand and re-emerged into the venue, where I noticed in the corner a small refreshments table. Grabbing the attention of the serving girl and having assured her in the strongest possible terms that yes, I was supposed to be here, I requested a large Scotch and parried her initial objections by insisting it was for a purely medicinal reason (i.e. I had severe bollock problems and the pain was making me blind in one eye). Eventually, and to my enormous relief, she found some of Mr Bells' special pain killer in the back room and provided me with a reasonable measure, along with some small towels to mop my face, neck and hands. The tumbler of medicine seemed at first to quell the worst of the agony, taking the edge off the shooting pains in my thigh, but seemed to do nothing for the rampant gut pain which I began to suspect was something to do with last night's garlic prawns. Sadly, there was little time to reflect on whether or not I had been sabotaged by the waiter at last night's Chinese restaurant, who seemed uncommonly surly at being called 'Ping Pong', because none other than Sir Jackie Stewart was now entering the room, to the obvious delight of the 30 or 40 attendant guests. Though all of these people had a head start on me in that they were wearing correct-sized trousers, had relatively few bloodied towels around their hands and were unencumbered by a ballbag that had now assumed the size of an agonising grapefruit, I was damned if I wasn't going to have my time to speak with Sir Jackie John Stewart. Accordingly, I made my way towards him as Kenny Heron led him through the room and made clear as I came near that I was ready to engage with a loud clearing of the throat that immediately escalated in a most unexpected way. Sir

Jackie Stewart left almost immediately, as did I, though only one of us was in an ambulance.

As I said at the start of this chapter, being a motoring journalist can sometimes lead you to meet a range of celebrities, and most of them aren't worth engaging with for longer than it takes them to sneer "You seem to have gravy on your forehead." Not so 'smiley' then, were you Carol? But it's also true that you might, one day, get to meet someone you have long admired from afar and, for that reason, you might, in the final reckoning, consider this a 'perk' of the job. Whatever else I might say about so-called 'stars', I can certainly say that Sir Jackie Stewart is, without question, the greatest celebrity I have ever vomited upon.

# 13. BECOMING AN AUTHOR

For the established motoring journalist, writing a book is a logical step on from seeing your name in newspapers, magazines and local court reports. The benefits of writing a book are that it gives you a longer format over which you can showcase your talents/earn more money. The book, then, provides the ideal way to develop an idea, share a passion and/or clear a gambling debt.

I must, however, issue a note of caution. Do not assume that, just because you find a particular subject interesting and you have a publisher who is going to publish it, other people will share your interest and flock to snap up a copy of your weighty work from online book sellers such as Amazon or physical retailers like the local Waterstones before it closed down. For every bestseller, there are hundreds of utter failures. Or, to put it in simpler terms, for every Why Oh Why Oh Why? by Jeremy Clarkson, there is at least one The History Of The Great British Roadster by Steve Easby, motoring correspondent of the Scarborough Sentinel. Apparently, he's still got them stacked in his garage. His wife has to crawl over them to reach the chest freezer. That's why they say the only man-made objects visible from space are the Great Wall of China and unsold copies of The

History Of The Great British Roadster by Steve Easby. I suppose you could say it serves him right for being a miserable git with a limp who tells a fellow motoring scribe to "stop doing that bloody Italian accent" during a Fiat press conference in 1989. Anyway, if Steve's lesson teaches us anything, it's that book publishing is bloody difficult and could make you look like a right tit who lives in Scarborough.

If my caution above sounds severe, it's there only to remind you that books inhabit a tough world. Trust me, I've been there, done that, got the T-shirt. It had a picture of local historian Anne Cleaves on it and was an impromptu gift from my publisher after some of my own clothes became wet and torn and then wet again.

The plus side of writing a book is that, as I alluded to above, you might receive a four-figure payment for your travails and this might be of particular benefit to your "balls", specifically with regard to them not being "ripped off" and inserted somewhere else, e.g. "your throat". Bad Gary certainly runs a tight ship, debt-wise. Thankfully, in my case, a book payment earned me a reprieve from his teste rearrangement schedule, and it was with no small irony that I remembered the long-standing local rumour that he can't read!

A book payment is often referred to as an 'advance', which, as the name suggests, is given to you before you've done any work and which can be converted immediately into cash, placed in a Spar bag and taken down to the Royal Oak where Gary's friend Catshit is waiting. Do not ask him to explain his name. Another note of caution; you will not receive the entire payment for a book in one go. Typically, it is split into chunks, the simplest of which is as follows: 33.3 percent upon signing of contract; 33.3 percent upon delivery of the finished writing (or "manuscript" in publishing speak); 33.3 percent upon publication. There are, of course, variations upon this, such as: 33.3 percent upon signing; request for 33.3 percent to be returned upon discovery of incomplete manuscript and/or missed deadline; argument about whether existing, unfinished words are "drivel"; further argument about where 33.3 percent of money has gone; legal case 'Lanchester versus Little Barn publishing of Huddersfield'; publisher decides to get someone else to see through their idea; money given to Steve Easby of the Scarborough Sentinel.

If my first experience of publishing taught me one thing, it would be that there's another door out of the cellar in the Royal Oak and it pops up in the ladies' toilets. The other thing it taught me, however, was the importance of having an enthusiastic and supportive publisher. That's exactly what I found in Len Fettis of Lima Foxtrot Publishing of Wetherby, with whom I published my noted work How To Pass Your Driving Test With Roy Lanchester. To this day, I maintain that writing the entirety of the words on the front in the same size and colour of typeface made the title a little mis-leading, but this a minor quibble.

My relationship with Len started in 1992 when he was very much a one-man band. By this, I mean he ran his publishing company largely on his own and not that he performed musical numbers whilst activating an implausible number of instruments at once, though he did once fall through a display of drums whilst attempting to blow a stolen trumpet in the music department of Fennimore's department store in Leeds after one of our legendarily long lunches! Despite the small size of his company, Len had enjoyed considerable success with a child's mathematics book featuring a certain leggy brainbox from the television by the name of Miss Carol Vorderman. First published in 1989, this work had been an unexpected success despite the poor typography on the cover, which made the title appear to read How To Add Up Carol Vorderman. After several reprints, and a less confusing cover design, it had become a massive hit and earned Len a tidy sum, only some of which he had to share with Carol, which rather undermines the idea that she is good at maths. Nonetheless, despite his unforeseen success, his overheads remained low and his thirst for the next big project remained high, which is where yours truly came in.

I should say right now that I believe any successful book starts with a good idea. In my case, the idea was to write a book in order to acquire a lump sum of cash to help settle irksome legal bills resulting from previous attempts to write a book/dispute the meaning of 'all you can eat'. One day, I was browsing the shelves of Cormorant Books in Harrogate looking for inspiration when I bumped into Len for the first time. It was immediately clear that he admired the cut of my jib, and, in particular, the way I was using some of my jib to store a small hip flask of Scotch. It also turned out he recognised me from my page in the local paper, and my various appearances on other pages, and when he identified himself and his company, I was proudly able to say I owned one of his books on local walks. I didn't mention that I had taken it by mistake from the Herald office and that I had no intention of using it, especially since it seemed rather too occupied with actual walking, often on routes that didn't go past pubs. Anyway, Len struck me as a good man, not least for his suggestion that we continued our discussion in The King's Head across the road with no shilly shallying pre-amble about whys and wherefores and what time in the morning it was. As soon as the pub opened, we sat down and got to business.

"Let me ask you this, Roy", Len said directly. "What do all of us have to learn to do in our lives?" I could tell he was going somewhere with this, so it didn't really matter that I answered "stain removal" and then wished I'd given a different answer.

"Three things we all need to learn how to do in life", Len continued. "S.S.D." He paused for a moment to let my expression become one of intrigue. "That's right", he said triumphantly. "Swimming, shagging and driving." I began to realise that Len might be a genius. "And here's where you come in, my friend", he added, lighting another Benson. As I sparked my own smooth cylinder of tobacco, I attempted to counsel Len that I was not a strong swimmer, much though buoyancy was on my side. "Bollocks to that, I bet you're not much cop at shagging neither", Len quipped. "You sound like one of my ex-wives!" I jested in return, and was about to continue with the important proviso that, during the entirety of our courtship and marriage, my second wife was an undercover lesbian and, therefore, unqualified to pass comment on my abilities between the sheets, but Len was already speaking again. "Driving, Roy. I bet you know your onions there. So look, I want to publish a book about how to pass your driving test, and you're just the man to write it", he said, before draining his beer. Immediately, I was struck by something. It was Len's palm slapping me cheerfully on my back as he got up because he was "busting for a piss". But while he was gone, something else occurred to me; he was absolutely right. Not about needing a piss, though I had no reason to doubt him there. No, he was absolutely correct about learning to drive. It was something almost everyone did at some point in their lives. Every week, there were dozens, hundreds, thousands, maybe millions of people all deciding to take those first fumbling steps into the world of legally harnessing a motor vehicle. Although probably not millions, realistically speaking. If a million people applied for a licence every week, that meant that, within a year, almost everyone in Britain would have requested a driving licence, including many children, and that would suggest a worrying level of fraud. No, if this book was to work out, it would be better to concentrate on the people legitimately applying for a licence to drive and ignoring those who perhaps just wanted a 'backup' licence in the name of Barry Singh to keep for emergency situations such as their real licence being taken away again. Yes, it seemed Len was on the money with this one and no mistake, something I wasted no time in telling him once he had returned from the lavatories and secured us another pair of pints. On the spot, a deal was done: I would write a comprehensive book on passing your driving test, Len would publish it and I would get us a couple of whisky chasers!

I must add once again that, if you are considering writing a motoring book, you must have a strong idea and not simply some old crap about British roadsters which no one can be bothered to read or, indeed, write. A simple, clear idea with sales potential is where it's at. As long as you have that, and as long as you remember to give yourself plenty of time to write it and not, as can sometimes be the case with book deals forged in pubs at 11:45 in the morning, agree to do it all within a month, you will be on to a winner.

To my eternal regret, How To Pass Your Driving Test With Roy Lanchester had several problems beyond a needlessly specific-sounding title. These issues began at the writing stage when I received regular telephone calls from Len asking to meet up for a "progress report". It's always nice to have a supportive publisher and I particularly enjoyed Len's idea of 'supportive', which was to meet in a pub of his choosing to have a quick chat about the book and then, as he put it, "get smashed". You will often hear writers talk about their way of working and, for me, this method worked extremely well, though, in retrospect, it was a little light in areas such as writing and arguably a little too heavy in other disciplines, such as somehow waking up in Nottingham.

Like anything involving the written word, books have deadlines and having missed the crucial date on my first ill-fated book project by one or two years, I was determined not to make the same error again. Happily, Len had invested some of his Vorderman fortune in the new world of desktop publishing and, with his permission, I was able to take layouts fresh from his hired designer and input new words directly onto the computer screen just days before the book went to the printer. Again, with the power of hindsight, it is easy to see that a larger publishing house would have employed a team of proofreaders and lawyers to check over such work. Of course, a larger publishing house wouldn't have been based in a shed in Len's garden, nor would they have rushed through most of the pages and sent them straight off to the printer while the head of the company was 'accidentally' on a ferry to Rotterdam.

These may sound like excuses for what happened with How To Pass Your Driving Test With Roy Lanchester, but I feel they are part of the explanation for why the book had to withdrawn from sale and all remaining copies destroyed. More specifically, these are the reasons why there were a number of problems with the finished product, which were highlighted in a terse rejection letter from a major retail group, a copy of which I still have. Their quibbles included:

– Bad or misleading advice, some of which could be dangerous, e.g. p56 "If in doubt, just pull out."

– Apparent endorsement of drink driving "in moderation".

– Gross defamation of Nigel Mansell (p34, p55, p67–72, p99).

– Needless use of profanity, e.g. p98 "The motorway speed limit is 70 mph, but even the cops will admit that's horseshit."

– Repeated endorsement of a Mr Ken Coates and the KKC Driving School of Harrogate, including several mentions of this business as "number one" and "the only driving teacher you should use" alongside Mr Coates' business telephone number.

There were several more of these, but I couldn't be bothered to re-type them. My point is this; publishing a book is hard, requiring time and an attention to detail that you may not realise, especially since the people who sell books are surprisingly pedantic about things like a factually accurate speed limit for residential roads.

My final piece of advice would be this; newspapers and magazines are temporary and, by their very nature, throwaway items. One minute they are fresh and new; the next you are taking them to the tip or using them to wipe up because you're out of toilet paper again. Books live for much longer and it is, therefore, important to get them right. With that in mind, always get someone to read the entire thing before it goes to print and make sure they don't simply scan over the first twelve pages and then leave the manuscript in a cab on the way to Hull.

I must confess, my experience with How To Pass Your Driving Test With Roy Lanchester was as unfortunate as the typography on its cover. Worse, it adversely affected my relationship with my publisher Len Fettis, to the extent that, after a heated debate over the money and why I couldn't return it, we didn't speak until long after the premature withdrawal and destruction of all known copies. This was, I should add, a bad time for Len since, at precisely the same time as the How To Pass Your Driving Test fiasco, he was poised to publish a long-awaited new kids' book by Carol Vorderman entitled COUNT! and found it a real blow when most retailers and customers took offence at the cover, arguing that its main graphical device was flawed and that Ms Vorderman's head was in no way an adequate substitute for the letter O. At great expense, a special sticker was applied to existing copies to make them less offensive, but the damage was done, plus it made it look like Carol had been decapitated. Understandably, it was a tough time for old Len and this perhaps explains his unfriendly behaviour when we finally spoke again by chance some years later.

To sum up, publishing is an extremely tough and uncompromising business and not to be entered into lightly. Not unless you want to be called a "fucking bellend" and then attacked with a ring binder in the Harrogate branch of W. H. Smith.

# 14. PHOTOGRAPHERS

In the world of motoring journalism, one thing goes with words like horse goes with carriage and failed goes with marriage. I'm talking, of course, about pictures. I'm sure anyone who has been a long-time connoisseur of the motoring press can recall a favourite image used to illustrate a story, whether it was a full-chested 1970s woman leaning on a Triumph TR7, a Ferrari poking from behind a haystack in the 1980s or one of those modern action shots where most of it is out of focus. I must add that words are clearly the most important part of any story, since they have all the facts and numbers in them and you'd basically have to be an idiot just to want to look at pictures, but I will admit that photographs play an important part in showing you what the car looks like.

Unfortunately, for many years, securing good quality photos of a car to go alongside the words carried with it the irksome need to engage the services of another person. That is to say, a snapper. A smudger. A lensman. I'm talking, of course, about photographers. If you're not familiar with this breed, let me tell you that you will rarely meet a more grumpy group in your entire life. Spend any time with one of these so-called 'professionals' and I guarantee it won't be long before you hear one of their classic catchphrases, such as "the light's not right", "this location isn't working", "I'm not sitting next to you on the plane back" and so on. Quite the demanding fellows they are, always wanting to get up early "to catch the sunrise" and then becoming unreasonably stroppy when you don't make it down until a civilised time like 9:15 am, or sitting in the passenger seat droning on about "backgrounds" and "visual interest" and telling you to "apologise to the waitress from last night". What a bunch of whining winnies they are! To cap it all, once they find a spot to get some nice shots of the car, they'll insist that you help them clean the bodywork and woe betide you if you claim you're busy having a smoke or being sick into a bush. Then they'll use up an hour of your valuable driving time taking detail shots of the gear lever and moaning (again!) about "the light" or "the angle" or "the smell" and pretending to twiddle their settings when it's pretty obvious they just leave it all on auto and then make a fuss to seem more important.

I was very lucky that, in my years on newspapers in the eighties, I rarely needed the services of a snapper, as we just used stock photos. However, all that changed in the nineties when I found some parallel outlets in the world of glossy, high-end magazines, such as Yorkshire Style, Yorkshire Splash, Yorkshire Stance and Your Extension. In those days, these upmarket magazines demanded top quality snaps for their pages and would typically book some freelance lens jockey to come with me on a chosen press trip, at least until they ran out of people to ask. It was, I don't mind admitting, a great inconvenience. When one is assessing a new car, one does not want to be weighed down by a sullen snapper in the passenger seat demanding to stop every two miles to have a look a derelict brick wall or rusting tractor and carping on about the "stench of booze". Worse yet, these pillocks like to make out that their job is difficult when I'm absolutely certain that it is not, unless there is something particularly hard about putting on a pair of combative trousers and carrying an unusually large bag. In my experience, all you need to be a professional photographer is a one-syllable first name and a camera. Then, you simply park the car in a field, apply a little bit of steering lock, snap away for a couple of minutes and get out of the way. Yet, they seem determined to frustrate and irritate with their cries of "I need my light meter" and rude barks of "stop puking there, you're in shot".

Fortunately, the professional photographer is a dying breed. Literally. At least one of the snappers I worked with in the old days has snuffed it, and perhaps that will teach him to eschew interior driving shots for Business Hotel magazine on the Fiat Stilo Multiwagon launch in 2003 because he claimed the journalist looked "too sweaty". No, the pro-smudger's days are numbered and this rather neatly proves my point that photographers are people who have always been a waste of time and money and were only there to hiss "Jesus, haven't you had enough?" across the dinner table. Modern technology has rendered them redundant, hopefully literally. Today, a completely untrained person can take a perfectly good photograph of a car using nothing more than a pocket camera or the lens built into their mobile telephone, radically shaking up the industry's approach to photography and quality. To my mind, this is a breath of fresh air, as the results that can be achieved with a compact camera are easily good enough for the increasingly low standards of the industry, and if one takes a step up to an affordable SLR, the shots can be highly impressive, even more so if one has a chance to download the contents of the memory before being forced to throw the camera into a ditch while fleeing from a pissed-off gypsy.

For me, however, the technological revolution, coinciding with the slashing of magazine and newspaper budgets, isn't just about proving that photographers have been over-charging on their day rates and huffing about trying to spoil everyone's fun. It's also about a simplification of the very important process of reviewing new motor cars. By way of illustration, let me talk you through how a typical overseas car launch used to work when you were forced to take a snapper with you. This is a theoretical situation, just to give you an idea of what was involved back in those days. First of all, you tell the magazine that you have been invited to drive an important new model from, say, a Well-Known Japanese Manufacturer and the event is taking place in, for example, Majorca and you suggest that this is what you will write about in, for the sake of argument, their June issue. The magazine agrees but then later rings you back – no email of course, this is April 1993 – and says they want to send a snapper and have booked someone called, let's say, 'Ian'. Then, later, they ring back and say that 'Ian' won't do it because of what happened on the launch of a Well-Known German Luxury Car the previous year and has passed on a message to say that I still haven't paid him for the damaged jacket. The magazine says that it's okay because they have now booked 'Pete', who I have not worked with before but who I am assured is "really laid back" and "not at all like other Pete", who, I am reminded, "still can't face Spanish food because of you". I take down this Pete's details and then telephone the Well-Known Japanese Car Company, who say they will book him an aeroplane ticket and a hotel room and then remark that I haven't worked with him before, though it's not clear how they would know this. As you can see, this is already a considerable amount of admin and we haven't even got into the airport lounge yet!

Two weeks later, Pete and I meet for the first time at the airport, I say it's nice to meet him, he says he's sure what he heard can't be true and we get onto the aeroplane, where he very soon marks himself out as typical of his breed with various complaints, which make it abundantly clear that we have very different opinions on topics such as armrest usage, drinks orders and the ethics of removing one's socks on an airliner. As you can imagine, the atmosphere has already become slightly frosty by the time we touch down in Majorca, and this is before he has used a single frame of film – no digital photography remember, since this is still 26th April 1993. From the airport, we decamp to the hotel and have just 45 minutes to go up to our rooms for the standard 'five esses' (shit, shower, shave, second shit) before it's back downstairs for a technical briefing. Except 'Pete', like most snappers, doesn't attend such things, leaving muggins here to persevere through it, and it's not as if he's doing something sensible like sitting in the bar, oh no, he's outside in the evening light taking detail shots of the car! I can see him through the window, behaving like head girl of the photography club. But, miraculously, when dinner is served, he's able to come back inside, and when I make this wry observation about the strange correlation between work stopping and five-course meals being served, he rather rudely says, "It's gone dark, Roy." Alright, I snort, there's no need to turn on the photographer's lingo, at which I can tell the other people around the table are secretly laughing inside. Pete seems in no mood for light-hearted banter, however, and spends most of the meal nibbling delicately at his food and sipping away at a glass of water, a bloody rude slap in the face for our host's bountiful hospitality which he only compounds by loudly suggesting that I "reign it in for God's sake". It's another problem with these snappers I should have mentioned; they have never understood how the industry works. This might also explain why 'Pete' rounds off the evening by taking exception to my affectionate impersonation of our Japanese friends, lodging a noisy objection to both my accent and facial expression. He then rises from the table with the words, "For the record, Pearl Harbour wasn't a person", and delivers the classic photographer's petulant demand; "In the car for 6 am tomorrow, I want to get into the hills for early light." "Haaa!", I roar as he minces off in his fashionable training shoes.

As is typical with these lens boys, you should have heard the fuss that 'Pete' made when I met up with him in the car park the next morning. "Blah blah fucking stink blah blah three hours ago blah blah grossly unprofessional", all in a shrill whine. I should have mentioned earlier that 'Pete' in this story is, let's say, Australian, and that makes him even more, for example, annoying. We are due to fly out in the late afternoon, so we don't have long to test the car and it's vital I drive it before writing about it, because I'm not making that mistake again. Unfortunately, 'Pete' has other ideas and, after some needlessly personal observations about my appearance and odour, he insists on driving us at some speed up into the hills where we can park, in his case the car and in my case the breakfast. So it goes on, all bloody day, driving for a bit and then stopping to appease the unreasonable photographic demands of a man who thinks it acceptable to call a journalistic colleague a "stinking arsehole". Eventually, we must head to the airport and, at last, I get some time behind the wheel of the Well-Known Japanese Car, enough that I can form some conclusions, one of which is that I am going to be sick again. As we pull onto the airport concourse and 'Pete' jumps out of the passenger seat to speak with the representative of the Japanese Car Company, I am forced to make a small and discreet vurp into the nearest receptacle, and then we are relieved of the car keys and ushered into the terminal building. 'Pete' makes it clear at the check-in desk that he does not want to sit "anywhere near" yours truly, and we do not see each other again until we are on the plane, at which point 'Pete' begins screaming down the aisle at me like a lunatic until the stewardesses ask him to please stop yelling "Fuck you Roy! Fuck you!", as it is unsettling other passengers. This, I'm sad to say, is just a typical example of what used to happen whenever one was forced to take a photographer in tow on a car launch. They are very difficult people and prone to completely losing their temper just because they've found someone else's sick in their rucksack.

Fast forward to the present day and you will note that, if I was to be invited on a press launch, I would simply turn up with a small camera or my mobile phone in my pocket and no troublesome grump in tow. I have done this in the past and here is how it works. You drive the car, you stop in the gateway of a field, in a lay-by overlooking an attractive vista or where the car has come to rest in the river, you snap off a few shots yourself and the job is done. Then, you head home, upload these pictures to your computer, email them to the magazine or newspaper, ring the art editor and have an argument about what constitutes 'in focus' and then, if he's still being a bloody idiot about it, simply use some off-the-shelf stock photos of the car that the manufacturer gave you on a memory stick. Job done!

Yes, in my time in the world of motoring journalism, many things have got worse, such as the quality of launches and the number of invitations I receive to them, but a few things have also got better, and one of those is the ability to dispense with the nuisance of photographers. I must say, I am personally delighted to be rid of them by dint of technology, progress and not having any high-end outlets any more!

# 15. CELEBRITY TOO

I talked earlier in this book about celebrities and the disappointing meeting thereof, as they reveal themselves largely to be grasping idiots full of entitlement and snotty "I was hoping there might be some soup left for me" self-importance. Well, there wasn't, Aled Jones at the Birmingham NEC Motor Show. Perhaps you should have tried to be more of a so-called Christian about it. What I didn't mention is that, when you become a motoring journalist, you can become a bit of a celebrity yourself, but hopefully a good one like Sir Jackie Stewart or TV's Steve Berry, who once lent me a promotional pen with 'Bosch starter motors' written on it and then didn't ask for it back, as he shouldn't, since I'm certain he didn't pay for it. I must confess, I have had my own moments of celebrity over the years, as is inevitable when you have your name and face in the local newspaper every week for years, and also write a car review column for them. It's easy to forget that, when you write for a living, there are people who hang off your every word, and I'm not just talking about lawyers for the local carpet showroom just hoping for another slip-up. I said sorry, we printed a retraction, it's worth noting that, while my allegations weren't proven, they weren't disproven either and probably won't be unless we dig up the whole of the car park, so let's just all move on shall we? Note to legal – have now removed reference to 'missing wife' from this para.

I've lost count of the number of times I've been minding my own business in The Three Sheaves or the bank or the bar that's where the bank used to be when someone has come up to me to ask a question about some car review I have recently published. "Should I buy one of those?" "Is it better than a so-and-so?" "His wife's gone missing, show some fucking respect." And so it goes on. These are the perils of being quite a 'known face' in the Harrogate area! I like to think that I am not just a familiar face but also a trusted one, and people know that I mean it when I say a car is good value or a rear wash-wiper control is well designed or some CCTV evidence is inconclusive. Being something of a local 'celeb' has other advantages too; I used to be afforded the odd 'bonus meat' in the local butcher, for example, at least until he took exception to something I said about the mk3 Nissan Micra, specifically, "It has come to rest in the front of your shop." As befits a local 'face', I was also permitted to run up a larger-than-standard tab in a couple of local hostelries, a perk I enjoyed until, eventually, I was asked to clear these slates. On this front, I very quickly learnt that celebrity is not to be abused unless you can very quickly lay your hands on 14 grand. That's the downside of being famous in the North Yorkshire area. That, and becoming verbally abused in a branch of Millets by a humourless carpet salesman's brother calling you "twatto".

However, there are other pluses to being a local celebrity and one of them for me was being a guest of honour at the inaugural Spofforth Cavalcade of Cars. The year was 1995 and I was at the height of my powers in the local news, both for my incisive reviews of landmark cars such as the mk3 Volkswagen Polo and also for my front-page dispute with local neighbour and even more localised idiot Wes Hester over the alleged damage to his alleged bungalow. In this era, it was quite the fashion for car enthusiasts in small towns and villages to organise officially sanctioned get-togethers and shows on village greens and school playing fields as a sedate and civilised reaction against the 'boy racer' trend of the day, in which youths would gather in fast food restaurant car parks to rev their engines, smoke their tyres and call me "that fat twat out of the paper". I'd love to return the favour by throwing a chicken nugget at your dad's plumbing business, Jamie, but I hear it's gone bust. As a civilised antidote to those idiots who got their news and pornography requirements from Maximum Power magazine and its ilk, the good people of Spofforth decided to put on a summer fair, the centrepiece of which would be a cavalcade of glorious old motor cars. They also decided that there was no one better to commentate on this spectacle than TV's Quentin Willson, at least until they discovered that his fee would be a little more than they were willing to pay, plus VAT, at which point the organisers got in touch with me through The Herald and asked if I would do it for £100. I said it would be my honour, asked for £150 and eventually settled on £105, plus the promise of free food and refreshment on site. I am not one of those 'stars' who makes ridiculous and unmanageable demands, as you can tell, and my only other request was just before the event itself, when I had to insist that the large Spofforth Cavalcade of Cars promotional poster outside the Oxfam in Harrogate be cleaned or replaced, as someone had obscured some of my name on it with the word 'ANUS'.

The day of the cavalcade duly arrived and I fetched up on site in plenty of time to size up the lay of the land, and I don't mean the organiser's wife (although there were some pretty strong rumours about what she was doing with at least two of the Otley men's choir around that time). A quick stroll around the well-arranged site showed that it boasted ample catering, plenty of bins and the promise of a good day for all. As I waited for one of the vans to finishing cooking another burger, I recall thinking that this was a simple, pleasant day out that most so-called celebrities would sneer at, and that it certainly promised to be an improvement on the last local fair I had attended, since there seemed to be relatively little chance of goose attack.

As the crowds continued to swell, I moved on, via the refreshments tent, to the organiser's office in the nearby church hall and, being careful not to do any choir singing in case I got sucked off in a red Vauxhall Astra in the lay-by next to the Esso garage, I spoke with the organiser himself, local teacher Paul Ball, about my duties for the day. "You're judging the car show in 20 minutes", Ball huffed, "so please don't have another one of those." I could tell he was stressed out, so I did as requested and, back at the bar tent, only ordered a half to see me through until five minutes before judging began. Cometh the hour and one of the stewards ushered me into the 'arena' area of the main field, which was basically a big circle of bales with some old cars parked in it. On one side was a small caravan, which I recognised from the Batley fireworks display as belonging to the local Round Table and which was used not for awful self-catering holidays but as a sort of commentary booth, currently occupied by local DJ Bobby Starr (real name, Pete Piddington), who I was familiar with, not least for a disagreement we once had about which parts of his girlfriend it was acceptable to grab when falling down some stairs. The format for this portion of the afternoon was simple; I was to walk along the line of ten classics in the company of local used car dealer Frank Hampson, someone I was also familiar with for reasons relating to both halves of a Ford Orion, and we were to award each car a mark, at the end of which we would tot up our scores to find an eventual 'winner'. As we approached the first car, an immaculate MGB, resplendent in bright red paintwork, I pointed to Frank and quipped to the proud owner that he was in good hands if he should wish for his mileage to be 'adjusted', something the grumpy Hampson did not find amusing. In fact, after hissing some baseless allegations about what I might like to do with paintbrush cleaning fluids, he gave me the silent treatment like some kind of cut 'n' shut girl's blouse. Charming! Unfortunately, his silence was more than covered by the irksome chirping of the idiot Piddington, yapping away over the PA system from the comfort of his caravan. It's quite the mark of the man that he used his access to a powerful speaker system to broadcast some banal remarks about the weather, the time and how sweaty I was, but, conspicuously, didn't mention anything about how he was sacked from Silk 1078 for taking promotional records and selling them to a second-hand shop on the parade. Nonetheless, I am a professional and it was my professional duty to walk along this line of old cars and say which one I thought was the best, even if I'd basically lost interest by the end and just gave top marks to the MG because it was the first one I saw. With judging done, there was just time to have a quick argument with Hampson about whether or not his son-in-law's Triumph TR4 was a "shitter", before I popped my head into the public address caravan to say "hello" to the DJ, then had a brief but heated chat with organiser Paul Ball in the refreshments tent about the sensitivity of the PA system's microphone and why people at a family event did not want to hear loudly broadcast phrases such as "put a fucking sock in it, Piddington".

Having been briefed on the foibles of the PA system, I grabbed a quick plate of hotdogs, another pair of pints and headed straight for the caravan to take on my second duty of the day, which was replacing the buffoonish local DJ on the microphone, giving the crowd a welcome break from the inane chatter that got him booted off the afternoon slot on North Yorks FM. With the main mic firmly faded down, there was just time to exchange some views with Piddington about who was or wasn't a "cocklord" and then I faded up the broadcast system again as the main event of the afternoon was about to begin.

As promised in the title of the event, a whole cavalcade of cars would now drive through the arena, featuring the classics from earlier plus a whole range of less immaculate but no less enchanting old cars following in their wake, all named and described by yours truly. Anyone who has ever attempted such a feat of live commentary will surely know that it is harder than it looks, especially if the people who booked you didn't make it clear that you were supposed to walk up the hill to the holding pen and get details of each car from its respective owner, something I would happily have done if I had known about it, it wasn't hot and I hadn't been busy getting another hot dog and have a dump. Sadly, the organisers were keen to get things moving and there was no time to gather info, but I wasn't concerned as I was a professional motoring journalist. After all, I wouldn't have been in my job if I couldn't correctly identify, say, an Austin Princess entering the arena and then be able to deliver my assessment of the car and its driver. Some 30 cars must have passed before me on that hot Saturday afternoon and I'm proud to say I never ran out of things to say about any of them, save for two brief pauses while I took 'comfort breaks' in the caravan's integral toilet.

Of course, no matter how accomplished your light-hearted freestyle commentary, there will always be those who don't see the funny side of your witty quips, and one of those people was organiser Paul Ball, who saw fit to enter the caravan as I was wrapping up by making the international gesture for 'cut your throat'/'shut it off'. Having complied with his request, assuming it was the latter, he dispensed to me a list of gripes, claiming that it was "ridiculous" to spy my pal Glen Kenward from the Post Office and use the PA system to ask him to secure me another brace of pints, that some of the car owners were "rightly angry" about my assessments of their cars and/or wives and, in particular, my use of the phrase "seen better days", and that my command of the public address system fader controls was "useless", informing me that I had unwittingly treated the large crowd to an unexpected "piss and fart show" during at least one of my much-needed bog breaks. Ball concluded his graceless attack by having the audacity to call me "a lazy, drunken amateur" and, while I can take any amount of 'feedback', I will not stand for that sort of slur on my good name and the very name of motoring journalism itself, something I made clear to him before exiting the caravan.

Of course, this is just one of the pitfalls of being a celebrity. You can do the best job possible in difficult circumstances, but there will always be others who only want to snipe and sneer at your station in life and, as a familiar face, you simply have to accept this with no real right of reply. Although, in this case, it turned out the caravan mic was still live and my replies were broadcast to the entire fair. Perhaps, for this reason, I was not invited back the following year and, while I'm sure Tony Mason did a decent job in my place, I bet he did not create the 'buzz' and 'talking points' that I achieved for the Spofforth Cavalcade of Cars with my loudly broadcast rumours about what the Batley Singers did to the organiser's wife and where!

# 16. RADIO ROY

Television is a dead duck and the internet a fad, but there is something noble and important about good, old-fashioned radio, though I rarely listen to it myself, as the music is always awful and the BBC stations are entirely manned by communists. However, I still believe radio has its place in the world and, in 1997, yours truly had his place in radio, as I was hired for a regular motoring slot on prestigious local station Yorkie FM, "broadcasting the length and breadth of the Yorkshires". It was a role I saw as a natural extension of my written work. That said, not everyone is cut out for audio broadcasting, as some people do not speak as they write. Richard Fissten of the Staffs Express, for example, has a terrible stammer that rarely comes across in print.

Anyway, back to 1997, which, you may recall, was a mixed bag as years go. In the plus column, the Ford Puma was launched and sheep cloning was finally made possible. In the minus column, Princess Diana died and jug-eared stealth socialist Tony Blair somehow wangled his way into Downing Street. Also, I was diagnosed with diabetes, which, on balance, had both pluses and minuses.

What you might remember from 1997 is that it was the height of a refreshing 'banter' culture typified by Loaded magazine and, under this fashion, before it was swiftly quashed as always by the PC killjoys, it was okay to drink lager beer in the daytime and look at boobs with abandon.

To reflect this cultural change sweeping Britain and irritating, champagne-sipping Guardianistas in their Islington ivory towers, Yorkie FM decided to launch a Saturday afternoon show with a distinctly 'laddish' theme, and I mean that in a positive way, not in the way Germaine Greer would say it because she didn't like men looking at a girl TV presenter's bare arse, the sour cow. The new programme, dubbed 'The Man Zone', launched in the summer of '97, hosted by the station's excitable sports reporter Danny Salmon, who helmed the show and led the gang of in-studio banter merchants for the first two months until, in a fit of over-exuberance, he inexplicably shouted "TITS!" live on air at 5:15 pm and was summarily dismissed, as he was already on a warning for calling film reviews contributor Greg Lemming a "nipple". In incidents like this, you could feel the claws of political correctness closing around the nation. Mind you, Salmon always struck me as a bit of a loose cannon, by which I mean a prick, and he later got done for stealing some After Eights from a petrol station, which rather suggests that there was something wrong with him.

Salmon's replacement was Ricky Fish, another young man with a loud speaking voice and a propensity to shout "wah-hay!" as a term of approval, both qualities that The Man Zone clearly required. Of more relevance to your correspondent is that Fish was quite a car enthusiast (even though he drove a

Toyota Supra) and one of his first moves upon taking over the show was to suggest that the regular slots on films, computer games, technology and football should be joined by a weekly segment on cars, which is where yours truly came in.

I was alerted to this new requirement by a pal at the station and took it upon myself to phone Fish himself to offer my services. Once we had got past his initial surprise at how I'd gotten his home phone number since he was adamant he was ex-directory, I moved on to pointing out why I was right for the job, which is to say that I had a wealth of experience as a motoring journalist, I had regular access to press cars from manufacturers (with a couple of exceptions) and I lived relatively close to the station's studios, which were in Leeds. I also added that I was quite the experienced radio broadcaster, having acted as a pundit for various local radio stations on multiple car matters. I thought it needless to add that much of this work had dried up after the humourless fools at the Northern News Network had booked me to comment on the BMW takeover of Rover in 1994 and then lacked any sense of humour whatsoever over my affectionate tributes to the new owner's accents and, more specifically, my suggestion that they had "annexed" Longbridge to create more "lebensraum". These joyless ninnies shut me down just as quickly as the po-faced buffoons at Radio 4 back in the late eighties, all because their little lefty brains can't handle a good-natured tribute to the Japanese accent, even though we were discussing Toyota building a new factory in the UK and, therefore, it WAS relevant, despite what the snotty woman said at the time. This depressingly serious approach had really put me off radio, but I had accidentally heard The Man Zone a couple of times when it had been on in the car, or the off-licence by the pet shop, and their brand of on-air larking around led me to believe they weren't the type of show that wouldn't hiss "your attitude is appalling and your breath smells offensive" to someone just because they had made a whimsical remark about "the Austin Auschwitz", and it was for this reason that I tracked down Fish and offered forth my services to his programme. To my delight, the following week, he got someone to ring me and invite me on to the following Saturday's broadcast for a "trial run" at an all-new motoring slot.

I had always believed that radio was a natural medium for me as I consider myself to have an excellent speaking voice, it being deep and mellifluous and with the right level of Yorkshire accent, which surveys of the general public always show to be something that people like, especially in Yorkshire. Frankly, I don't know why more companies don't base their call centres in God's own counties rather than in stupid places with an utterly incomprehensible accent, such as India or Wales.

Another reason I was naturally drawn to the great broadcasting medium of radio was my experience on television, which, as already mentioned, I found to be deeply disappointing and short-lived, whereas in radio you have no fear of the old adage, "the camera adds ten pounds and more sweat", which I found to be particularly apt where my face and neck were concerned. With these issues banished, the audience is left to focus purely on a person's voice and the words they are speaking, which is another appealing facet for a wordsmith such as myself, and their appreciation is unaffected by what you look like, unless they have read about you in the local paper in one of the reports with a photo by it or seen the byline photo next to your motoring column, which I had repeatedly asked them to change, as it made my head look very bloated for some reason.

So it was that, in August 1997, I travelled to the Yorkie FM studios to make my debut appearance as the motoring expert on The Man Zone and was met in reception by the show's producer, Sanjeev something, who was Asian. Fortunately, I was already aware of this, having spoken to him on the phone in order to agree what they would like me to do on the show, which was to provide a short spoken review of a new car and three or four motoring news stories, plus the option of answering a couple of listeners' car queries on the phones if there was time. "I warn you now, it's August and everyone's away, so we don't get a lot of callers", Sanjeev cautioned, as we walked through to the studio. "But when it's quiet, it's a good time to try out stuff that might not work", he added, presumably referring to whatever japes Fish had planned for this programme.

The Man Zone occupied the crucial 4–7 pm slot on a Saturday afternoon, aiming to provide some welcome banter for men who had finished watching sports or being dragged around the bloody shops by their wives, not that this was a problem for me, as I have no interest in soccer and my last wife at this point had run off to become a lezzer! The first hour of the show was largely dedicated to sports, as Fish and his 'posse' of in-studio hangers-on debated that day's results and took calls from a series of largely inarticulate men who had been drinking heavily. After the 5 pm news, the show then became more interesting as a broader range of interests were discussed and it was in this section, at a scheduled time of 5:30 pm, that I was to deliver my first motoring segment. Accordingly, I was ushered into the studio some 10 minutes beforehand, while Fish debated some recent film releases. It was a room in which I felt immediately at home, though I must confess that, when entering the live studio, I did break the old radio rule about not falling over a chair and then saying "SHIT! Shit! Sorry!" After this minor blip, however, it was all plain sailing and I don't mind admitting that I was in my element as I delivered a typically witty and irreverent review of the SEAT Arosa, even managing to parlay Fish's daft attempts to call it the 'Arouser' by suggesting that it would be ideal for his wife, which was a perfectly amusing thing to say at this time, as I didn't yet know she'd run off with his brother.

All-in-all, my debut appearance on The Man Zone was a great success and one that wasn't diminished at all by making the host of the show hiss "just fucking leave it" during a jingle and then dash out of the studio crying, nor by our only caller for the 'car advice' segment turning out to be my irksome neighbour Selwyn Prees, calling up to moan about my bloody collapsed car port, as usual. Sanjeev Producer clearly agreed with my assessment of my first appearance, as he telephoned the following week to say that they would "cautiously" like to continue with my motoring segments for the time being, as long as I would "apologise" to Fish. In general, I maintain a zero apology policy, but I was delighted by the idea of a regular radio slot and felt that this warranted a small sorry, which was duly delivered the following Saturday whilst Fish was outside having a cigarette during the 5 o'clock news. With that minor problem dealt with, and another brief apology delivered the following week because Fish didn't look particularly Jewish which I why I didn't realise, all was smooth sailing and 'Lanchester's Motors' became a fixture of The Man Zone for the following weeks, entertaining the Yorkshire area, helping it with its car buying dilemmas and ignoring its criticisms that the car reviews were "just being read out from the paper".

As I said earlier, you really cannot beat the spoken word for gravitas, even when Fish's irksome sidekick 'Oggy' keeps shouting "OOOOH!" over your report on the Daewoo Leganza. Sadly, however, and as the saying goes, all good things must come to an end, usually when you accidentally back a Volvo C70 into their stupid Supra. So it came to pass that my working relationship with Ricky Fish gradually soured to the point where, perhaps inevitably, he was in the car park of the radio station shouting "You fucking idiot" at me. The decline towards this moment was gradual however, and began with a series of incidents in which Fish seemed determined to take offence at my remarks. You see, though his on-air persona was loud and extremely lively, I soon noticed that, off air, Fish was a most gloomy individual, at least some of which seemed to be related to the whole situation with his missing wife. "Listen mate", I once said to him, "my wife walked out on me and you don't hear me moping on about it the whole time." But this had no effect and, in fact, led him to accuse me of being "unprofessional", just because we were on air at the time. There were other issues too, such as me telling the annoying 'Oggy' to shut his face, though I'm certain that this request was supported by many listeners and advertisers. Typically, this supposedly 'wacky' character soon showed a total breakdown in 'zany humour' when I started calling him 'Ian' on air, even though that was his real name. I wonder how many of the audience would have played along with his 'antics' if they'd also known he was the type of man to corner someone in the radio station toilets with the words, "Just stick to the fucking on-air name, right?" Yes, it seemed Mr so-called 'Ian Ogmore' was the kind of a low quality wedding DJ who didn't want Yorkie FM listeners to know about it. Unfortunately, he was also good friends with Ricky Fish, as they had worked together since they were both at Scarborough 1057 and, as a result, they operated in league together to undermine me and my role on the show, leaving other team members Dingbat Dave and The Beer Monster very much caught in the crossfire. In fact, I think this latter pair were on my side, since I once saw Monster (real name Richard Moon) in The Cross Keys in Harrogate and he didn't disagree when I said Fish was a miserable tit. Sadly, Dingbat and The Beer Monster were mostly in the studio to make whooping noises and were powerless to stop the fool Fish and his little bum chum from engaging in idiotic behaviour, such as activating annoying sound effects from their side of the desk when I was talking or playing a jingle when they knew full well that I hadn't finished my last sentence.

Asian producer Sanjeev could not control them, since he had left four weeks after I started, to be replaced by Becky Lester, who was no help and wholly unsuited to the job on account of being inexperienced and a woman. If she wanted to be taken seriously from the off, she could at the very least have referred to herself as Rebecca. Anyway, this was Fish's show now, and that made my position untenable, even before I cracked the bumper on his crappy Toyota. In truth, things were probably beyond saving after the moment a couple of weeks earlier when, as he cued up an ad break with the words, "we'll be back soon", I was unable to help myself, adding, "unlike your missus". At the time, I didn't think he could get any angrier, though the lightly damaged Supra soon proved me wrong on that score.

I left my slot on The Man Zone in November 1997 in less than ideal circumstances – i.e. being told on air that I was sacked – but with some fond memories of my time in the marvellous medium of radio. I like to imagine that, in my short time on Yorkie FM, I brought pleasure to the listeners. Though some complained that I was just reading out my weekly newspaper reviews, the mere act of reading them out gives them a very different feel, plus it was ideal for people too stupid and/or lazy to read the paper. I believe it can be all too easy as a motoring journalist to stick firmly in your rut of the written word and I feel proud that I made a brief but successful move into the world of the written word that is being spoken.

As for Yorkie FM, in 1998, it was rebranded as Y!, which was also what listeners said at the time. This re-launch saw the station move towards courting a more female audience across the board and I'm delighted to say that meant the end of The Man Zone and the termination of Ricky Fish's reign of terror. When the failed Zone was broken up, I gather 'Oggy' decided to focus on his wedding DJing and The Beer Monster went back to just being a music technology teacher. I don't know about the other two sidekicks, or care. As for Ricky Fish, he ended up getting the drivetime slot on Sheff FM, in Sheffield, I gather. He later bought a mk2 Toyota MR2 and was convicted of assaulting his brother outside a nightclub in Hull, both of which rather proved my original belief about him, i.e. that he was a twat. Still, his personal failings are no reflection on the medium of radio, which I still look back upon with fondness. Indeed, if anyone is looking for a professional broadcaster in the field of all matters motoring, then it's something I would very happily return to, assuming we could agree a suitable fee!

# 17. THE JUDGE

The start of the year 2000 was a memorable one for me. The so-called Millennium bug turned out to be nonsense and yet more proof as to why we shouldn't trust supposed 'experts' (although I'd already had to throw away my toaster for other reasons) and the working landscape was looking buoyant for me as I'd just picked up the motoring gig at Loft Extension magazine. But there was something else significant about the start of 2000 in Lanchester Land because, in January of that year, I returned from Thailand with something new, and I don't mean herpes this time! No, I came back from a short sojourn to South East Asia with a brand new wife! Her name was Sukhon and she was, at the time, a delight, being far more attractive than a British woman of similar spec. This felt like a new era in my life. A fresh century, a new wife and no need to throw away any of the DVD players I'd been given on launches.

On top of all this, there was something else afoot in my world as, early in 2000, it was confirmed that I was to be one of the UK judges for the EuroCar Excellence Awards 2001, a prestigious pan-European prize given by a range of respected motoring journalists from across Britain and the Continent.

Normally, I might have dismissed this as the kind of nonsense one now hopes Brexit will banish, but I had been talking to Tim Horsewater from The Reading Century who had got himself a place on the voting panel for the 2000 awards and he reported that the assessment and selection process for the winning car involved very intensive use of some excellent hotels and restaurants. With this in mind, I wasted no time in putting myself forward for the 2001 panel once I heard a space had opened up thanks to recent amputee Phil Longhead from The Newport Sentinel, who had resigned on account of suddenly having fewer than the required number of legs.

Sporting a new wife was a tremendous boon when it came to the EuroCar Excellence Awards, as many of the events related to it included an invitation for a spouse and it was positively encouraged that she attended. The EuroCar people seemed very keen on this, perhaps to deter any of the judges from being benders, although there were some pretty strong rumours about the chap who joined the UK panel in 2004, no names, no pack drill!

The EuroCar awards worked in a way that was very simple but also rather like the EU and, therefore, terrible, which is to say that representatives from across Europe met up and the Germans told us what to do. They would work closely with all European car makers to compile a comprehensive list of all new models coming up in the next 12 months, which was, of course, highly confidential and should not be repeated in a British regional newspaper column, as it turns out. This list would then be whittled down by the ubergruppenfuhrers in the Fatherland to six finalists, which were meant to represent a spread of car types, and these contenders would be announced to us as we all met for the first time that year at a secret location in Frankfurt, which, disappointingly, turned out to be a hotel right next to the airport. Indeed, such was its proximity to the flight home that the other four British EuroCar judges foolishly elected to jet in and out in a day, whereas I made it abundantly clear that I would be staying the night, especially as Fiat was picking up the tab for this one. Hold on, you might think, why was Fiat paying for a journalist on an awards committee to have a steak dinner and some drinks and taking care of an invoice for a damaged hotel piano? Isn't that rather close to bribery? Of course it isn't, for Fiat was not even on the shortlist for the 2001 award but had scooped the previous year's gong for its Multipla and was, as EuroCar custom dictated, funding the first meeting of the following year as a 'thank you'. Though, as I pointed out to their Italian PR chap at the meeting, another way of saying thank you is with laptop computers, as you will often find that at least one of the members of the press in the room has discovered his is broken because of some wine that got inside it.

Anyway, in late February 2000, we had this Frankfurt meeting to which wives were not invited, something I was thankful for, as Sukhon had already complained that British towns and cities were 'dirty', which was a bit rich considering the shithole she came from. Nonetheless, I didn't want her to see Frankfurt, which, in my experience, rarely suffers from litter, dog turds and 'SEX TORIST' [sic] sprayed on someone's garage door.

In the large lecture hall of the hotel's conference centre, the president of the EuroCar kommand committee announced the six cars we would be focussing on this year, some of which had yet to be announced and would not be available to drive until several months from now. However, that was fine as, in my experience, condensing too much driving, wining and dining into a short period can have dire consequences, and even lead one to suffer a terrible wave of nausea in an airport security queue, with various unfortunate knock-on effects. No, this would be a long, drawn-out process, much like explaining to a Danish airport security man why you have put a bag of sick through his X-ray scanner.

As had been outlined to me late one night by Tim Horsewater, and then again the next morning when I could remember it, the EuroCar award was considered so important that car makers would grant the judging journalists early access to their newest models and lay on special events for all 50 of us, five from proper countries like Britain and two or three from the less important ones, like Portugal. I remember thinking at the time that this was going to be an interesting, not to say sacred, task. So, let judging commence!

My EuroCar odyssey began the very next week, when I was taken to drive the Peugeot 607 in the South of France in the company of my new wife. This was quite a blessing, as she'd already started to moan about the weather in North Yorkshire as if it was somehow my fault, so a trip to warmer climes was just the ticket to shut her Thai trap up and all for no expenditure on my part. We were staying in Les Trois Collines near Nice, which I had enjoyed once before on the Renault Mégane mid-life refresh event some years earlier, though I was perturbed to discover that, in the intervening period, they had expanded the premises and introduced a 'health spa'. I do not fully enjoy any hotel that boasts of such facilities, as they inevitably make at least some of the building smell of chlorine and vastly increase the number of wet idiots wandering around in dressing gowns during the daytime. On the plus side, the 'spa' gave me somewhere to stash Sukhon for the day, and this negated the need for her to come with me in the car, which, instead, I could do alone. We dined well on both nights, I recall, with the coq au vin being a particular highlight and my new wife was generally well behaved throughout.

March 2000 was even busier for judging, as there were two cars to consider, the first being the new Volvo V70. The Swedes offered to send an early production car in left-hand drive straight to my house, but I quickly reminded them that this was simply unacceptable. "Do I look like I live in a high quality hotel for at least two or three nights?!" I quipped to the PR man. Joking aside though, it is less than ideal when trying to assess a car for something as important as the EuroCar Excellence Awards to find oneself sitting on the 'wrong' side of the car when driving. Thankfully, Volvo fully understood this and hastily flew some of us to Sweden, where we were hosted in a splendid hotel outside of Stockholm and treated to a particularly delicious roast elk on the second night. As a bonus, we were also taken to view Volvo's state-of-the-art safety facility, which meant a third night's stay, this time in a reasonable hotel in Gothenburg. Looking back on my notes for the V70, I see that I had elk again but it wasn't as good as the previous night. A black mark for an otherwise excellent car. I didn't take Sukhon on this trip as she was still moaning that it was cold in Harrogate, even though it wasn't, and Sweden would have only made this worse. It was bad enough that I returned home to find she had been running the central heating pretty much constantly, racking up a bill that I probably couldn't charge back to Volvo.

March also saw a trip to Germany to sample the new Mercedes-Benz C-class and, on this occasion, Sukhon did come with me because, as I said before, the EuroCar awards people seemed quite insistent on bringing wives into it, no matter how much of a nuisance they were. As you would expect from Mercedes, our hotel was very well put together in every regard and the food was of a high standard, especially the veal. The British view of German cooking is pretty much the opposite of the British view of German cars (i.e. we think it's not excellent), but I've always been quite happy with their emphasis on sturdy, meat-based dishes, though I hasten to add that I still won't touch their wine unless there's nothing else left! Looking back at my notes from this trip, I see that the car was "excellent" and also that we were taken out in powerboats, those interested went off skiing (no such nonsense for Lanchester; I have found plenty of other ways to break my knee) and that the intensively meaty diet caused a 'failure to deploy' in the toilet department on day three (though it all came good on day four). All in all, a delightful five days away, spoilt only by my bloody wife, who spotted the full-figured manager of chassis systems for the C-class project at the breakfast buffet and loudly shouted, "He even greedier than you."

There was then a merciful break in the judging process, during which I could return to the 'day jobs' and also to my increasingly frustrating home life. Yes, living with Sukhon was not panning out the way I had hoped at this point. In fact, my new bride was proving to be disappointingly useless when it came to wifely duties, e.g. ironing, cleaning, sex stuff. In addition, her cooking was bloody awful, especially as everything she made was basically just a thin soup with shit in it. I recall one evening around this time, gently suggesting that this evening's meal could be a pie or a nice lamb chop, but when I returned from a trip to the tip, she was already busy in the kitchen shoving unidentifiable vegetables into a pot of brackish water as usual.

On a brighter note, late May saw EuroCar business take us to Italy to sample this year's entry in the medium hatchback class, that being the Alfa Romeo 147. One can always count on an Italian event to lack the ruthless organisation of a German equivalent, but to make up for it with a mushroom ravioli in truffle oil, which was so delightful that I later rang down to the reception and asked them to send some more up to my room, much to Sukhon's disgust! She was probably confused because it wasn't swimming in spicy rainwater! As well as their cooking, the Italians are known for their hospitality, which, on this occasion, took the form of a briefcase containing a laptop computer. At last, you might think! Sadly, I had already been forced to buy a new computer of my own, but this new one was of a better specification, so I kept it and sold the other one to a man in The Red Lion when I got home. That laptop lasted for years, unlike an Alfa 147 one might add, though at the time I found it excellent and gave it top marks for allowing me to spend time at the event location, which was Lake Como, a natural wonder that is always a pleasure to see, smell and later fall into.

The following month it was off to Basque Country to drive the new Citroën Xsara Picasso. Noting the name of our destination and its similarity to an item of women's clothing, I quipped to Sukhon that she should "dress appropriately", but she did not pick up on my clever wordplay and was also barely speaking to me at this point. We had fallen out several times just before this Citroën trip, the final straw being when she insisted on coming to the pub with me, something I knew she was doing purely to irritate me and so that she could wait until I was about to order another pint or Scotch and then shout, "You have too much already" in that annoying way of hers where she didn't pronounce all the letters properly.

Nonetheless, the trip to sample this practical new family car was, in places, an enjoyable week away, with a chance to experience an area I was not familiar with and to stay in some generally decent hotels, La Casa de Verano near San Sebastian being a particular highlight. I had the hake.

Towards the end of our stay, a Citroën PR approached me and announced that he would like to give me a gift as thanks for joining them to drive the new Xsara Picasso. "Is it an actual Picasso?" I quipped! But, in fact, it was just a fancy coffee maker and a case of wine.

The rest of the summer was quiet for EuroCar judging and noisy in my house on account of Sukhon listening to her bloody awful pingy-pong Thai music and shouting ungrateful things like "you fat stupid" at me, even after I had pointed out that there is no such thing as "a stupid". At the end of August, it was time to sample the final entrant of our six and the representative of the small car class, which my European colleagues kept referring to as the Opel Corsa, though I insisted on using its proper name, which is Vauxhall Nova. I took great delight in saying this every time I heard someone on the testing event in Barcelona use the words "Opel Corsa", until some of the German contingent became rather shirty with me over this, and also a couple of other things. The first was an accident, and, besides, tables can be replaced; the second was not an accident, but then I always say that if you can't laugh about it then don't start a war in the first place.

Our accommodation on this trip was generally first rate, though the hotel on the sixth night as we headed up to look at the Corsa factory in Zaragoza was disappointingly only four star. In the plus column, I must admit that, though I generally find tapas too fiddly and too small, it was served on more than one occasion on this trip and, generally, I enjoyed it, even if it sometimes became tiresome having to ask them to bring more, especially when addressing those kind of Spaniards that pretend not to understand English. I should add that the wine throughout was just like the car (i.e. excellent), although I was never told that I'd had "more than enough" of the car! As I made clear to these interfering Germans, and also French and I think some Danes, if I wanted to be told to throttle back on the booze, I would have brought my bloody wife, which, thankfully, I had not!

Some months later, representatives of the car companies with models on the shortlist assembled at the same hotel conference centre in Frankfurt where we judges had met at the start of the year and the winner was announced to them. Unfortunately, as a result of the Vauxhall event that encompassed Barcelona, Zaragoza and, in my case, a local police station, I had some ongoing issues with several of the other judges and a few of their wives, and I was not invited to the secret announcement ceremony. I should add that the reason the manufacturers are informed early is so that they can begin the process of printing the stickers, brochures and such like which will celebrate and publicise the win, such is the importance of what is almost certainly Europe's second or third most prestigious automotive award. The lead time also gives them a chance to send out to each judge a case or two of 'thank you' wine or a 'thank you' television. Sadly, I did not receive such a gift, though I later discovered it was a 'thank you' watch and a 'kind regards' weekend for two at a very good hotel in Paris. My failure to receive these polite tokens of gratitude could be blamed on the bad blood between myself and 70–80 percent of the other judges. For the same reason, I only discovered the winner when it was in the press and I can't be bothered to look up what it was in the end, though my memory says the Ford Mondeo, which is weird since we didn't even drive that. No, my association with the EuroCar Excellence Awards was very swiftly wound up in what I liked to refer to these days as 'Royexit', as I was able to regain sovereignty over which cars I reviewed and which hotels I stayed in.

Mercifully, by October of 2000, I was also free of my terrible third marriage, having agreed that I would pay for Sukhon to return to Thailand and never contact me again, save to finalise divorce proceedings. Happily, it later turned out that my Thai bride and I were never legally married in the first place, thus saving me a fortune on lawyers, though, of course, I was still out of pocket overall.

So, I had been a judge and then decided to get sacked. I had been falsely married and then ducked out of that one for the price of a plane ticket. I had finally got my idiot neighbour to admit that the death of his cat was mostly not my fault. Yes, the year 2000 was quite an eventful one for me. Oh yes, and I had to throw away my kettle in the end, not because of the Millennium bug, but because some nagging Thai idiot had tried to cook an egg in it!

# 18. LONG-TERM TEST

One of the terms you may have heard bandied around in motoring journalism is 'long-term test'. It was certainly a phrase my local newsagent picked up on a few years back, possibly because I had used it, and he asked, quite reasonably, what it meant. Unfortunately, as I was explaining in more detail, I was hit with the effects of an unusually potent mid-morning livener I had enjoyed en route and fell unexpectedly into a display of crisps, prompting him, quite unreasonably, to ban me from his shop. His loss, since I never fully explained what 'long-term test car' really meant. Well, in return Mr Chattergee, you are banned from reading this chapter of my book. Also, I saw your nephew smoking marijuana around the back of your shop in 2004. Plus, I still have your invoice for £8.56 and I can assure you I will not be paying it, especially since I see you have closed down your shop nine years ago and the chap in the fishmonger says you died. Looks like I'm up on that particular deal, eh?

So, back to the 'long-term test car'. Quite simply, this is a press demonstrator given to a journalist for an extended period of time, longer than the typical loan period of a week and as long as a year, or perhaps even greater if you can successfully claim to have misplaced the car and can fend off the people from the manufacturer until they discover that you have sold it. Now, you might be thinking that being given a free car for an entire year sounds like nothing more than a tremendous perk, but you would be wrong about this. It's only by having a free, fully insured, top-of-the-range car for a year that a journalist can delve more deeply into all aspects of this model and discover things that would not be immediately apparent or impossible to divine over the course of a mere one-week loan. Does the car use more fuel than claimed? Will it need new tyres more often than expected? How easy is it to get stains out of the seats? Is the local dealer attentive and courteous, whether you have a minor problem such as slight damage to the bonnet or a major issue like accidentally running over one of their salesmen? These are the valuable insights that can only be gleaned by running a car for a year, and, of course, all such knowledge can be passed on to your readership, who will be better informed as a result of your experiences, the good and the bad. Although not too bad. You don't want them to take the car away early.

For much of my motoring journalism career, I avoided the long-term test car simply because I was in the business of providing new car reviews and, between the press cars and the regular launch trips, I simply had no need for another free car. Also, there was often no room on my driveway, especially as the car port remained in a state of collapse. All that changed, however, in 2002, when I began to experience some troubles with getting hold of regular press demonstrators. The excuses given ranged from the evasive ("we don't have any cars because there's a delay at the factory") to the more direct ("Thomas says you can't have another because of the amount of damage to the last one"). Happily, it was at this point that I encountered a friendly marketing chap from a little company called Kia who, back then, were an obscure marque who would lend me cars rather than, as today, a household name who won't. In those heady days of 2002, I would best describe Kia as a small but growing concern, with an admirable objective to engage with the media and then buy them lunch. So it was that the marketing chap put me in touch with his boss, a Korean gentleman called Mr Kim, although his first name might also have been Kim; I was never exactly sure and he never corrected me either way, not even when I introduced him to several people as 'Kim Kim'. In an engaging telephone conversation, some of which I could understand, Mr(?) Kim told me that he believed that, under his watch, the UK marketing department had to "think national but act local", and this meant it would be time well spent to convince the regional motoring media of their motor cars' merits. I let Kim/Kim carry on in this vein for some time before pushing him for a cast iron assurance that he was, indeed, offering to visit me and buy me lunch.

We met some weeks later at The Waggon & Horses near Lanchester Towers for an agreeable lunch, over which Kim (Mister) told me of his hopes for Kia and we discovered that we had several mutual interests, including a fondness for whisky, though our tastes differed slightly in that my Korean friend enjoyed a complex Highland single malt of an evening, whereas I preferred a serviceable Scottish blend while we were speaking. Another even more enjoyable piece of common ground was to emerge at the end of our lunch, since it became clear that we had a mutual interest in me having a free Kia for a year. "I think over a longer period you will be truly impressed with the quality and design of our company's products", M. Kim concluded in an accent that I was, by now, becoming quite good at understanding. Better yet, the car he was offering for my use was the flagship Magentis saloon, about which I had heard good things, although, in fairness, most of them were from Mr Kim earlier in the meal. I graciously accepted his offer to give me the car and, indeed, to pay for lunch, just as soon as I had secured another large Scottish wine. However, I had to warn Kim that I was not simply one of those journalists who would spout soft, fluffy, uncritical copy in exchange for a free car, and he seemed to accept that by smiling and nodding politely, though I began to wonder if it was now he who was struggling to understand me! I meant what I said, of course, but as it turned out, the Kia that was delivered to my house the following month was, in fact, excellent, something I was only too happy to make clear in my regular reports for The Harrogate Herald, such as the eight-month update reproduced here:

After eight months on the Lanchester fleet, the superb Kia Magentis continues to rack up the miles in and around Harrogate without a hint of trouble. The superb V6 engine remains as smooth as a sewing machine around town, while the pillow-soft ride soaks up our potholed streets as if they weren't there. On longer runs to Leeds-Bradford airport or across to Manchester Ringway, the Magentis continues to cruise arrow straight, while the silken automatic gearbox shifts ratios unnoticeably. Rear seat passengers regularly comment favourably on the comfort afforded to those in the aft quarters, while also making note of the impressive standard equipment levels for the price, and your correspondent continues to have no qualms about the comfort levels afforded to the driver, which are, quite simply, superb, with all controls falling easily to hand and no aches to be reported from the sumptuous leather-clad seats, even after many hours at the wheel. It is a tribute to the superb smoothness and comfort of the Magentis that it is a pleasure to be behind the wheel, even late at night on a run back from Knaresborough or Ripon. If I had any criticism of the superb Kia Magentis, it would be that it is unfairly overlooked in favour of flashier European and Japanese competition, though, of course, that is hardly the fault of the car itself. I would thoroughly recommend that anyone in the market for a superb compact executive saloon should try one out, or get into the back of mine!

Unfortunately, running a long-term test car was not without its problems. My reports appeared at least once a month in the paper and, though they seemed well received by some readers (e.g. a chap called Gillium Trist, although, in fairness, he was the local Kia dealer), they were less well received by some other readers, such as the people tasked with enforcing minicab licencing in the Harrogate area, who unfairly considered references to 'rear passengers', 'airport runs' and 'vomit clear-up' to be 'evidence' which backed up several reports that I was using my Kia as an illegal minicab. I strenuously denied this unfounded allegation of course and found it typical of the meddling, namby-pamby attitude of local government, forever interfering in the private lives of citizens who, yes, might occasionally give lifts to friends and who, yes, might sometimes take those friends and their luggage to airports and who, yes, might gratefully accept some petrol money from those friends whilst perhaps giving them a sort of receipt for the money in case they wanted a record for their files. There is nothing illegal in all this and the petrol money came in very handy, as I was experiencing some liquidity issues around this time after receiving a disappointingly poor return on some shares and also horses. I was also engaged in a rather sticky legal battle with the Little Chef restaurant chain and a running insurance battle caused by the irksome collapse of my front garden wall onto a Citroën. None of this was anyone's business but mine, and perhaps my solicitor's, and maybe my neighbour's for at least as long as he claimed the Citroën was still his property no matter what was on top of it, and I fiercely protested against the tiresome bureaucrats who sought to infringe my right to give friends a lift to Leeds on a Friday evening and then pick them up later in return for petrol money and a bit extra because I agreed to let them stop for a kebab.

My protests fell on deaf ears, unlike the ears of Kia, which were sadly dragged into this ugly battle when the mean-spirited buffoons on the local council discovered them to be the registered keepers of the superb Magentis and confronted them with their mealy-mouthed allegations. Not-Mr Kim seemed unamused by these baseless accusations and, since my year with the Kia was almost at an end, made steps to retrieve the car from me. This would have been a huge inconvenience since I had no other press car bookings forthcoming and, without the Magentis, I would have been literally without a car. This was especially unfortunate since it was coming into summer and, over the following two weeks, I had several bookings from friends who wanted me to drive them to the airport. I, therefore, parried Kia's rather brusque request to take back their car by claiming that it had been stolen, little expecting them to take my whimsical remark so literally and to do something as silly as report my claim to someone as interfering as the police. Following this irritating turn of events, and with my need for petrol money now at an all-time high following fresh allegations for what I had done in the Little Chef and into what, I decided to do Kia a favour and sell the Magentis on their behalf, fully intending that we could come to a cash settlement at a later date. This was to become a long-running matter of debate between the company and myself. I believe I did nothing wrong; they insist that the car was their property and that, therefore, only they held the right to sell it for cash to a man in a pub. In the end, they made such a fuss about this that the car was returned to them and the whole situation became one of the reasons I can no longer drink in The Viceroy's Arms.

To sum up, you might sometimes look at motoring journalists and think that they have a cushy life with their long-term test cars. Well, take it from me, this simply isn't the case. A long-term test car is, in fact, a huge hassle that will get you fined £850 by a magistrate's court!

# 19. PR

As a motoring journalist, there's one group of people you deal with on an almost daily basis, and I'm not talking about the police or those grumbling idiots who deliver press cars and then moan when you tell them they can't have a lift to the station because you've had too much writing wine and, anyway, it's only a 35-minute walk. No, I'm referring to PR people, not to be confused with Pierre Peepell, the Renault designer from the 1980s who became unreasonably surly after I enlivened his talk on 'innovative use of materials' by shouting "garlic!" several times during and after.

PRs perform a vital role in the car industry, that role being to hold open doors for car journalists on launches, check them into hotels, give them the keys to the cars and make sure there is a corporate credit card behind the bar. However, their job actually extends far beyond car launch events to other important tasks, such as booking in press cars, arranging the collection of press cars and speaking with journalists on the telephone, during which they must remember not to get needlessly angry nor use rude, unprofessional language, such as "and how did it get into a fucking river again, Roy?"

In my experience, PRs can be divided into two groups. There are the good ones, who are always full of fine manners and good cheer and for whom nothing is too much trouble, whether it's collecting a car from an unusual location or taking care of the bill for the damage to the roll-top bureau. Then there are the bad ones, who display poor courtesy and lack such basic respect for journalists that they will cling to a ridiculous grudge over a simple misunderstanding about some press car tyres which were accidentally transferred onto a journalist's wife's car and who will loudly tell an esteemed member of the press to "shit off" on the bus back to the airport after the Punto launch. I'm sorry to say, there are rather too many of the latter in this industry and these people would do well to remember that they are here to serve the motoring journalists, not to keep carping on about what did or didn't happen to the headrests from their stupid Nissan. These bad eggs are often the same misguided souls who believe it is their lot in life to exert some influence over the journalist by telling them that a new model is great rather than letting us decide how excellent it is after we have sampled the full launch experience and perhaps also driven the car.

As a layman, you may still wonder why the launch itself is as important as the attributes of the car. Well, as I have already explained, the quality of hospitality on a car launch is a great indicator of the quality of the car itself, just as the attitude of the PR person is indicative of the attitude of the company that employs them. If the second bottle of Petrus is not chilled, what does this slapdash attitude say about the car maker's ability to design a reliable cylinder head? If the PR man refuses to explain to the hotel manager that the number and quality of hookers in the journalist's room is none of his business, does that suggest the car maker is also happy to hire people who can't be bothered to design the brakes properly and just huff that "this is all your fault, as usual"?

You might be forgiven for thinking that automotive PR is easy, and, for the most part, you would be right, yet, still, this occupation seems to attract a worrying number of people who are ill-suited, sometimes literally. In order to illustrate my point, have a look at the questions below and ask yourself how you would answer:

1. A journalist on a launch has left his diabetes medicine at home. Do you a) insist he goes home to get it himself or b) take up the suggestion to fetch it for him as it's only a two-hour drive away, once you get to the airport at the other end?

2. A journalist was accidentally given the keys to the hotel's bridal suite and finds the room he is actually sleeping in to be disappointingly inadequate by comparison. Do you a) make him put all the bottles back into the bride's minibar and then physically bundle him into the slightly smaller hotel room or b) make the necessary behind-the-scenes arrangements to ensure the journalist can stay in the suite?

3. A journalist's trousers have become ruined by things beyond his control (i.e. geese). Do you a) point and laugh and loudly suggest that the journalist 'honks' in front of journalistic colleagues or b) quietly arrange for the journalist to take delivery of a pair of courtesy trousers?

If you answered b) to all of these questions, you could make quite a good car PR, assuming you're not one of those people who's going to start quibbling about 'panel damage' when I'm trying to book in a press car. If you answered some or all of the questions with a), then I'm afraid you are one of the bad guys and I'm pleased you got moved into internal communications at BMW, Neil.

There are rather too many of the bad apples for my liking and these unprofessional PRs often show their true colours when a journalist loses his high-profile gig on a national paper or steps down from a flagship regional title to spend a brief few months working abroad, whereupon the false smiles and agreements to cover the extra costs "on this occasion" are suddenly replaced by swiftly truncated phone calls and extremely terse letters about the how upset a female member of the press team was made by said phone call, whereas any decent PR boss would understand that, where I come from, it's a term of endearment to be called a "daft cow".

Anyway, I don't want to make out that all motoring PRs are bad eggs because there are also some eggs out there that, like Scotch or pickled, are good. My old mate Kenny Heron, for example, was a PR gentleman of the old school, although, ironically, schools were one of the things he wasn't allowed near after a ridiculous misunderstanding in the late nineties over some photographs found in his briefcase. Dear old Ken worked at various companies over the years, but no matter where he was employed, he brought with him a relentless enthusiasm, a sparking wit and a steady pouring arm. I recall being with him on a launch in Nice in the late eighties when we decided to take a pre-dinner stroll through the town, only to become completely lost! In those pre-smartphone days, there was no hope of digitally orientating ourselves, so we decamped to a bar, enjoyed a couple of bottles of navigation wine and then set off again, only to become even more lost than before! To make matters worse, yours truly then set off up a side street and realised that I had somehow become separated from Kenny and was now flying solo, and dinner was due to start in less than 20 minutes! Happening into a welcoming-looking establishment, I chanced upon a lady who spoke reasonable English and engaged her in conversation. Shortly afterwards, I glanced out of a window at the back of the building, only to realise I was looking directly at the front of our hotel! But, by then, I'd paid for half an hour with one of the lady's colleagues and dinner would have to wait! So you can imagine my surprise when I walked into the dining room late to find Mr Heron still wasn't there, and didn't appear for another 20 minutes, much to the consternation of his PR colleagues, many of whom were terrible bores and found tardiness unamusing, as they did things such as speeding tickets and bottles of Scotch charged back to the room. "I thought herons were good at homing!" I quipped loudly, which, of course, Kenny found tremendously witty. Then, the next day, they discovered some very specialised French magazines in his bag and he was asked to leave that particular car maker, but I'll never forget his face when he walked into the dining room to find me already there! It's a story I'll bring up with him one day if I visit him in prison.

Talking of the industry's PR good guys brings me on to good old Johnny Bauvais, who I'd describe as a real character, and not just because he often wore a bow tie. Johnny was at several car companies during his career before becoming a freelance PR consultant, and he approached every job with the same relentless bonhomie and sparking wit that made him popular with everyone, apart from the woman who got him sacked from a certain well-known car maker in the early nineties. I couldn't begin to count the number of bars I've propped up with Johnny around the world and, whenever I think of him, I always see his eyes twinkling as he grinned, "One for the road, squire?", which was something of a catchphrase for him, at least until he entered the clinic in the early 2000s. We became less close after his unfortunate drying out but I was still deeply saddened in 2015 to hear that Johnny had taken the last of the '12 steps', which was to die. It was a great honour to attend his funeral in Marlow, and to be sick on his surviving wife. They say that a good turnout at a funeral is a mark of someone very popular or very unpopular. I know I've certainly made an effort to turn up to plenty of funerals for utter shits just to make sure they were gone, but in Johnny's case, it was a mark of complete respect, widow vomit incident notwithstanding. I can only hope my funeral will enjoy such a good turnout of people who aren't just there to pretend not to be pleased. Not that I will be there to see it, of course, contra to the words of Sandy Badger of the Bolton Advertiser, who once muttered, "By 'eck, you'd turn up at your own burial if there were a free bar", which is a completely ridiculous suggestion since who would pay for an open tab at my funeral, apart from a well-known German car maker?

Other PR stars I should single out include Jack Lach, who was a gent to the last and never gave any hint of the crimes for which he was later convicted, Phil Gillot, whose unswerving dedication and flawless hospitality gave little indication of the alleged embezzlement that later saw him allegedly dismissed from what was allegedly a large European car maker, and Gareth Larm, who was always great fun, at least until he decided to become a gay, at which point he turned rather too flamboyant for my liking, though I should stress that he never attempted to bum me.

Unfortunately, over time, these favourable PRs seem to have become outnumbered and outranked by the jobsworth buffoons who seem to make it their aim to work against the experienced journalist rather than working with him and, if necessary, putting up a unified front against the Moroccan police. I've grown tired of the usual excuses for cancelling invitations to launches or refusing the loan of press cars, a list of which I've compiled below. Whenever you hear any of these, game over. You're dealing with one of the tiresome 'new breed' who don't understand how this industry works. Examples include:

- Event overbooked
- Limited availability on the fleet
- Prioritising long-lead titles
- Nick says definitely not
- Too much damage last time
- Can't afford to replace another interior
- Blacklisted at board level
- Appalling smell of faeces
- Rick wants you to return the other car first

I could go on. These moaning, politically correct ninnies have ruined the motor industry and will not stop until car launches are sanitised affairs conducted at wheat hemp smoothie bars in a wellness retreat with an emphasis on driving the car and talking about tampons. It's a nonsense that I can't abide and,

Frankly, I'm sometimes glad not to be invited on as many launches these days!

What makes the sad shift in the PR world all the more regrettable is that these pumped-up pompous oafs try to make out that their job is difficult when patently it is not. What is so hard about holding open doors and remembering the price of the entry-level model? It simply isn't difficult and I can say this because, in common with many motoring journalists at some stage in their careers, I once made the leap onto the 'dark side' by becoming a PR.

You may be surprised to learn that this happens a lot. An otherwise perfectly normal journalist decides that, for whatever reason relating to money, they cannot continue as a car scribe and forgo a life of claiming that a wide range of cars is excellent for a new job pretending that just cars made by a certain manufacturer are excellent instead. It's a fairly standard industry career path for people who insist they want to earn a living, though it's one I didn't expect to take myself, especially since Johnny Bauvais had once jokingly told me I'd be "fucking awful" at PR! However, in early 2005, after returning from a few months working abroad, I found that my usual outlets had, like Johnny himself, somewhat dried up. Money was a little tight due to all of it being taken away by the tax man and/or Jason the casual bookmaker, and I found myself in need of employment. Enter Laslo Jackson, a pal from my newspaper days and now the owner of LLJ PR in York. I mean 'now' in the sense of 'at the point in time I'm talking about' (i.e. 2005), rather than 'now' as in, 'as I write this'. That would be wrong as he's now dead.

Anyway, I happened to be chatting to Jacko as I once called him, and he immediately asked me not to, and talk turned to my employment, or lack of it, and my money, or lack of it, and my testes, or lack of them if some gambling debts were not sorted out. "I tell you what, Roy, I've just picked up an automotive account and we've got to organise an event for them", he said. "I need someone to sort some stuff and we're really desperate, so why don't you have a crack?" Needless to say, I told him to fuck off, then realised how broke I was and phoned back to say yes!

Don't-call-me-Jacko's new account was for up-and-coming Chinese van maker Waifeng National Automotive Concern (WNAC), who were launching in the UK and wished to make this fact known to the people who mattered; that is to say, journalists. Laslo's brief to me, after we'd got past his initial concern that, just 20 minutes ago, I'd told him to fuck off, was to swot up on the vans, find a place to host a launch, plan a driving route for the vans and then be on hand at the event to answer questions and generally do PR things, like pick up the bar tab, pay for the damage and assure the relevant journalist that no one else would find out about the piss-damaged mattress.

I got straight to work two days later by taking delivery of all the bumf on these new vans and began the process of digesting it that evening in the company of some high quality reading juice. Suitably updated on vital information like the names of these vans and news that they all came with an engine of some kind, the following day, I began to ring around some likely venues that could host our event. Having attended enough launches myself, I had the ideal location in mind; it would be a large stately home hotel somewhere in the north of England with plenty of rooms for guests and an understanding policy on superficial furniture stains. My first appointment was made for the following week, which was to investigate Hurstling House near Linton-on-Ouse.

Now, although PR work is plainly easy, I will admit that my lack of familiarity with this role did cause me to make a basic error on my first reconnaissance trip, which is to say that I hired a car, having been issued with a company credit card for expenses, and drove to the venue, forgetting that I would have to sample the wine on offer, the result of which is that I had to get a taxi home and then another taxi back in the morning. It was a good job I'd remembered to get out a load of cash on the company card! For my next possible venue, I did not repeat this mistake and got a cab there from the off, and for my third investigation, I hit upon an even better idea, which was to insist on a room at the hotel for the night, thereby dispensing with the need for taxis since I could leave the hire car outside, plus I was able to fully investigate the facilities, such as beds, lavatories, cleaning etc.

After I had checked out of my seventh and final potential launch venue, I wrote up my findings and paid a visit to Laslo Jackson to present to him my recommendations, only to find him in quite a foul temper and ranting about "bloody hotel bills" and "hundreds of fucking quid on fucking hire cars". Having assured him that I was not, as he claimed, "out of" my "fucking mind", I attempted to reassure him that I was merely being thorough, but this only seemed to make things worse. "Thorough?" he shouted, testily. "It's a Chinese fucking van. A fucking village hall would do it, you daft bastard." I began to understand why Mr Jackson had never found employment at a major manufacturer, since his PR manners were rather slack and his communication had been extremely poor up until this point. If he had not wished me to, as he put, "blow half the fucking budget" on my reconnaissance work, then he should have made this clear from the off.

Nonetheless, keen to make amends for this breakdown in understanding that was entirely his fault, I went away and found a newly constructed outward bound centre near Sproxton which had a hall for presentations, clean and simple rooms for journalists to sleep in and a large car park for the parking of vans therein, all at a very reasonable price. I even suggested that a local pub could cater the event, with proper pub grub, real beers and a selection of wines, which I would not 'test' without his permission. To my delight, Jackson was not displeased about all this, to the extent that we agreed to forget the five-grand bill for my recces and he endorsed all of my suggestions, apart from the one about hookers.

Now it was time to move forward with the next phase of the launch, which was to draw up a driving route for the journalists. For this task, Laslo arranged for me to take delivery of a brand new WNAC X8 2.0-3100 medium-wheelbase van in which I could investigate some likely roads. My first impressions of this machine were that it seemed attractively designed and well made, and that it was easy to drive, though reversing was somewhat impeded by the lack of rear windows and then a low wall. The route itself was easy, since Laslo had warned me that van journalists didn't need that much driving time and were more concerned with running costs and load capacity than handling or being able to stop for a drink. Accordingly, I planned a simple route out to Scarborough, up to Whitby, inland towards Middlesbrough, then down across the moors back to our base. As I suspected, all this PR stuff really was a piece of cake and the only thing left was the following month when we welcomed our invited guests.

Come the allotted time and I made my way to the outward bound centre, which, I must confess, Laslo's 'decorations department' (i.e. his assistant, Jenny) had done an excellent job of jollying up with bunting in the main hall, check-clothed tables and framed posters of vans. I helped to welcome the attendees in the morning, hand out van keys and keep an eye on the hired staff who were distributing tea and coffee. I must admit, I did find it quite annoying how many questions the journalists asked, but I was happy to address each concern by directing them to the press pack. I was also struck by how brusque and even rude some of the members of the press were towards those of a PR persuasion (i.e. me on this occasion). There followed a short talk about WNAC's ambitions in the UK, which I didn't really listen to, as much of this stuff was also in the press pack, then a light lunch and, finally, off went our two dozen or so guests in their vans. Again, this was something of a pain as it required some organising for which, I noted, the journalists gave little thanks. Indeed, some were extremely impolite when moaning about being given the keys to the wrong variant and what-have-you. As such, it was quite a relief when they finally all drove away on the route I had carefully written up for the launch booklet, apart from one major junction, which it turned out, I had forgotten. Anyway, that showdown was to come later but, for now, yours truly was left with little to do for the rest of the afternoon, so I busied myself helping the landlord of the local boozer, who was setting up his beer and wine behind the temporary bar in the corner, and then offered to sample some of his wares to be certain of their quality, which was excellent.

All in all, the launch was a huge success in my view. In Laslo Jackson's view, it had a few sticking points and I still have the letter he sent me in which he outlined some of those. His petty quibbles included 'welcoming guests back from their test drives whilst holding a half-drunk pint of beer, shouting "let's get on it"', 'staggering around the pre-dinner drinks sidling up to journalists and hissing, "It's a fucking lovely van isn't it?"' and 'attempting to lead our guests in a song of your own invention with the deeply offensive lyrics "ching chong China van"'.

Although I have little to no memory of these moments, they sound, to my mind, like incidents of great bonhomie and I'm certain the attending journalists were greatly entertained by a person in a PR position who took such a relaxed and fun stance, rather than some stuffed shirt droning on about load height or some such.

Fortunately for me, I managed to get some proper writing work again shortly afterwards and didn't have to ask Jackson for any more PR work, which was lucky because he made clear that he wasn't going to offer me any. However, my experience in the PR world taught me several things, the main one being that it's extremely easy and anyone in such a job who makes a fuss out of it is an idiot. However, it also taught me that, while PRs are often extremely annoying and prone to asking rude questions about how and why the chaise longue came to become broken, they are also a necessary evil in our industry. I'm sure in the future they will invent computers and robots that can sort out press car bookings, get you adaptor plugs from reception and find you a replacement shoe, but the human touch of a good PR is hard to replace, if not impossible. I suppose what I'm leading to is that, perhaps, I will miss PRs when they're gone, assuming that happens before I die. I know some PR offices have a sweepstake on this and I don't want to give them the satisfaction if possible.

To conclude, my experience in PR was an interesting one but not something I would wish to repeat, as I don't like being asked questions or shouted at by strangers. However, from it, I did learn the most valuable lesson of all, which was that, in future, I would take the time not to be rude to PRs unless they start it or there's a pre-existing situation (e.g. I already think they're a twat)!

# 20. THE MODERN PRESS LAUNCH

I wrote earlier in this book about the heyday of press launches, when no hotel was too luxurious, no wine too expensive and no staircase irreplaceable. Well, it saddens me to say that those days are firmly behind us. Of course, foreign launches still take place, ideally in a place that is sunny and expensive and where I'm still allowed to go, but these are distinctly muted affairs and I'm rarely invited, as a new generation of prissy and picky press officers prioritise vloggers and 'lifestyle' journos and people who would rather spend the evening in their room writing and making videos than letting off all the fire extinguishers onto Rex Huxstable from The Altrincham Argus.

These days, I find that the easiest overseas trips to get on are not new car launches but those junkets to the host manufacturer's new factory or research laboratory, and this is a much less attractive proposition, since these premises are rarely interesting or licensed. If I want to drive a new car and get a hotel room somewhere half-decent, I must attend one of the UK regional launches, which are, as their name suggests once you know what it means, designed for the regional press in Britain and take place on our shores, usually at some stately home or other, probably one that has been turned into a hotel, although don't take that for granted and be sure to read the invitation all the way down to the bit where it says "One-day event. No overnights" before you tuck into some of the hearty refreshments in your bag after the road testing is done. Take it from me, suggesting to the owner of a stately home that you will simply "bunk down" on the red sofa in the corner will be met with all sorts of mealy-mouthed carping about "Regency" this and "family home" that. Happily, the PR man on that particular event was persuaded to give me a lift home and it was no skin off his nose, since he only lives about 80 miles from me.

Personally, I've traditionally found the UK-based press event to have a couple of downsides. First of all, there's always the chance they've decided to base it just outside Harrogate (i.e. right near my house), with the attendant wrangling that requires to secure an overnight room at the hotel. The more professional PR will make no mention of this, but there are always those less refined members of the press office contingent who will greet you in reception with loudly jocular remarks such as, "Why have you got a room, Lanchester? I can see your fucking house from here!" Fortunately, he was sacked from Citroën in 2001. Yes, Bobby, I was one of the people who complained about you. In the old days, the other horror of a no-flying press launch was the lack of a chance to top up on duty free, a handy saving sadly erased on European travel thanks to those meddling bureaucrats at the EU. Meanwhile, I'm sure they were getting plenty of reduced-price cigarettes and whisky on their gravy train, no doubt.

Conversely, a UK launch does have some advantages. It affords the chance to get to know a car on the correct side of the road, it reduces the need to spend any more tedious time in the airport executive lounge and driving to the launch venue gives you valuable time in whatever other press car you might have booked that week, thereby killing two birds with one stone. Or, as happened to me on the way to the Renault Scenic facelift event in 1999, two horses with one Rover 45.

You might imagine that, upon arriving at a typical press event, even in the UK, the journalist would be carried aloft upon a sedan chair into the venue and plied with the finest Champagnes. Not so. There was a Daewoo event where they had sedan chairs once, but this courtesy was not afforded to yours truly amid some griping about weight limits. Don't assume the fine Champagne as a given either; there are plenty of times you have to demand it, and, even then, you may have to make loud observations about its quality before they'll crack out the really good stuff. I should add that I'm not usually that fussed about Champagne because it makes me fart like a tractor, but insisting upon a glass of it is a good test of a host's hospitality. Rest assured, I will be certain to scrutinise the engineering of a car made by people who respond to simple requests like this with inadequate excuses such as, "but it's ten thirty in the morning".

You might also imagine that the driving portion of a press launch in the journalist's home country is conducted entirely at his leisure and that he is free to take a car at will, drive it where he pleases and entirely at his own pace. Sadly, this is not the case. For one thing, the manufacturers would rather you followed their set test routes, provided in a booklet accompanying each car or programmed into the satellite navigation, and attempting to drive where you like is frowned upon, especially if it is across the lawn and into an ornamental fountain in a Daihatsu Terios. I've apologised for that once, so it's unnecessary to do it again, especially as I still believe it was totally pointless, both the fountain and the car.

Another bloody inconvenience of the modern press launch is that you are usually required to share a car with another journalist, a protocol that comes fraught with all manner of petty squabbles, internal politics and feeble cries of "But Roy, I don't want to be in another accident." Therefore, whenever one is on a press event, one has to choose one's driving partner very carefully. Is it, for example, someone whose company you enjoy and who won't suddenly shout "Oh DO shut up" halfway through the Peugeot 107 launch drive in Portugal? Ironically, the chap in question is the one who has now shut up, permanently – i.e. he's dead. Perhaps that will teach you, Stanley. The second thing you must consider in picking a driving partner is an even more delicate matter; do you trust them behind the wheel, especially for the afternoon stint when you will have had a couple of relaxants at the manufacturer's agreed lunch stop and will require chauffeuring at a stately pace back to the hotel? You might imagine that all professional motoring journalists are excellent and skilled drivers, but this is sadly not the case. In my view, many are overly cautious and do not push the car to its limits, thereby failing in their duty to analyse vital qualities such as on-limit handling, high-speed braking performance and, where applicable, crash safety. Conversely, some journalists are rather gung-ho and seem incapable of driving a car at anything less than full chat, even if their passenger is wasting good and barely digested Barolo out of the window and a bit into the footwell. Personally, I like to take a mixed approach, driving gently where appropriate but having no fear of bouncing off the rev limiter, and several other cars. After all, the whole point of testing vehicles is to push them to extremes and, with this in mind, I make no apologies for the odd bald tyre, overheated brake pad or unexpectedly entered supermarket. I make no secret of the fact that, over the years, I have pushed more than a few cars up to and over the limit, and also a dry stone wall. Indeed, my stance on this is utterly unapologetic, a fact I once had to make clear to a tetchy PR man in front of the entire restaurant on a launch after he attempted to pull me up for some superficial damage to one of his precious cars and a rectory. "Listen sunshine, your job is to provide the hardware", I boomed in front of the whole room. "Your problems are not my problems because I have plenty of problems of my own!" I concluded, at which I recall everyone in the room started applauding, even the waiting staff. This episode has gone down in motoring journalism folklore and I gather is regularly re-told to this day, though I suggest you ignore the versions which claim that I delivered the last line and then started crying.

Anyway, pairing up for driving on a launch event is a strange dance and you will always find that a certain portion of the other attendees do not want to partner with so-and-so or what's-his-name for whatever reason, often leaving one person who gets a car to themselves. This is not a problem, as I get the morning behind the wheel and then insist the PR drives me back to the hotel after lunch.

I do, however, have one other tale of caution from the UK launch circuit, and it's not the one about the intricacies of attempting to birth a turd into a corridor litter bin at 3 am. In my view, a certain well-known international hotel group should spend more time designing rooms that don't allow the occupants to become locked out during a nocturnal search for the bathroom and less time telling people they have been captured on CCTV and are banned from all their hotels for life. No, my cautionary tale comes from the BMW 1 Series mid-cycle refresh event at Brockley Hall near Shrewsbury in 2007. The day started normally as I awoke in the hotel, descended for a hearty breakfast, enjoyed a brief and lively debate with the hotel manager about the previous night's damage to his French doors and waiter, and then found a partner in Ken Kessler from the Glossop Sentinel, who I managed to corner in the lavatories before he had paired off with someone else. Dear old Ken had a marvellously dry sense of humour and responded to my partnering request in his usual laconic manner. "Oh Jesus, I suppose so", he quipped, "but don't bother talking to us because I've gone deaf." Priceless! Off we set on the agreed route, myself driving first and Ken lounging in the passenger seat chiming in with the occasional "Slow down you daft bugger" and "For fook's sake man, the level crossing lights were flashin'!" The car itself seemed little changed from its predecessor, always a tough one to generate a lengthy review for, but I had formulated a few angles in my mind, such as what it meant to be the only rear-wheel-drive contender in its segment and how this drivetrain layout affected its ability to recover from a brief loss of control while passing across the frontage of a garden centre. To the sound of some mild Cumbrian blasphemy from Ken, we arrived at the designated lunch stop in an old mill near Telford, explained the cause of the panel damage to the press car coordinator and then headed inside for a hearty lunch and, after a reasonably heated debate, a swift livener for yours truly. I was mid-way through the second bottle when a PR lackey made it clear to me that everyone else had left, including Ken Kessler, who had apparently paired off with someone else, the turncoat shit. "There might be another spare seat in one of the other cars if you hurry", the press lickspittle continued as I attempted to butter another bread roll. "But you probably should go now", he added. With a pointed sigh at his impertinence, I got up and headed outside, taking the bread with me. As I descended the steps to the car park, there was just a lone 1 Series left and it was already reversing out of a space. Noting that the front passenger seat was empty, I leapt in as fast as permitted by my bad knee and spastic anus to find at the wheel a mousey lady I had not passengered with before. Frankly, press launches are increasingly full of these pointless blouse enthusiasts, all writing for Women's Realm or Lady's Garden or what-have-you and needlessly protracting press briefings with stupid questions about the price of the car or the fuel economy and, therefore, delaying everyone from moving next door for dinner. I rarely find these women interesting or attractive and haven't wasted any effort in speaking to them, so I was unsurprised not to recognise this woman nor know her name; thus, I simply barked, "To Brockley Hall and don't hang around!" If this might sound terse, it was nothing compared to the absolute rudeness with which this lady set off without a single word and some rather heavy inputs to the BMW's controls. In my experience, these kind of people often grip the steering wheel too tightly, a habit that I find most irksome, as I believe the wheel needs only the lightest of grasps even when, to take a recent example, the car is moving rapidly across a meadow and it has become clear that the front wheels will take no further part in steering the car on account of having been removed moments earlier by a kerb.

Onwards we went in the 1 Series and, though I made a listless attempt at conversation with friendly bits of driving advice such as "try not make any sudden moves, love" and "if you relax, this will be so much easier", the rude woman simply stared intently at the road ahead and spoke not a word. Typical. In the face of such stonewalling, it is little surprise that, despite her hopelessly jerky driving style, I nodded off in the passenger seat.

You can, therefore, imagine my surprise when I was awoken some time later by a knocking on the window, which turned out to be a police officer who was in the area on account of us being parked outside a police station. There were, in fact, many police officers, all in the favoured mood of the police (which is, in my experience, aggressive disgruntlement) and loud exhortations were made to put certain things – e.g. "your hands" – in certain places – e.g. "where we can see them". "What on earth is going on?" I said to the lady from mousey woman magazine, except it became clear that she wasn't listening on account of no longer being in the car. In order to stop the police shouting at me, I stepped from the vehicle, only to find myself being aggressively spun around and pushed against the side of it before being frisked, insulted for the quality of my trousers (which I grant you were rather damp in places) and then bundled into the police station, whereupon a rather grumpy sergeant started barking at me using words like "threatening" and "against her will", to which I pointed out that, if a woman comes on a car launch, then she is hardly acting against her will. The puce-faced policeman became even more agitated and tried to claim that I was "kidnapping" the flowery lady "at knifepoint", a claim I stoutly rebuffed. There was some back and forth, after which it finally became clear that the weedy lady was not, in fact, a car journalist of any sort, even a terrible one from a womanly magazine. She was, it emerged, merely some civilian who happened to own a BMW 1 Series, who happened to be visiting the venue where we had stopped for lunch and who happened to be rather startled when I got into her car and instructed her to drive to Brockley Hall. "How would you feel if a huge man stinking of booze and brandishing a knife got into your car?" ranted the unreasonable copper, points I took issue with as a) my size is better summed up as 'burly' and b) I'd barely had a bottle and a half. However, the knife claim was a chin scratcher until I realised I had left the venue in such haste and with such a handful of bread rolls, it seems I had inadvertently brought the butter knife with me too and may have waved it casually in the feeble female's direction.

For once, the police agreed to release me without charge and, as I was leaving the station and about to telephone the PR man to ask him to pick me up, I encountered the mousey lady in reception and attempted to set the record straight, something the stuffy 'old bill' once again took exception to. In my view, this woman needed to toughen up, as she could be made to cry just by an innocent man saying, "Jesus Christ woman, did you think I was going to butter you to death?"

After a frustratingly long 45-minute wait during which I was mercifully able to shelter in the pub opposite the cop shop, the PR arrived in his 3 Series and we headed back to the hotel. I took the opportunity to caution this fellow on a failing with his new car and the subject of this launch for if I, a professional car journalist, was able to get into a pre-facelift version of the 1 Series and detect no difference from the facelifted model we had been dragged here to drive, perhaps there was something amiss. "You should report this to your Fuhrers in the Fatherland!" I noted, helpfully. "No", he replied in a sullen tone. "I won't be telling Germany about any of this." And they wonder why people think they have no sense of humour!

Unfortunately, a lack of sense of humour is a mark of the modern press launch and part of this problem is that the job of motoring journalist has changed if not beyond all recognition, then certainly enough that, upon visiting it in hospital, its own family would gasp and one of the weaker womenfolk would probably faint. Long gone are the times of week-long launches, after which you would be whisked home by private jet with a thoughtful gift, such as a case of wine or laptop computer for your troubles, before settling down to craft some careful prose about the vehicle you had tested at a thoughtful and gentlemanly writing pace. These days, launches, whether at home or away, are rushed and uncivilised, hurrying the journalists around like pieces of meat (although pieces of meat that can walk, i.e. cows), with no time or consideration for taking in breath or liquids. You often have to bring your own from home to be on the safe side. In the latter case, I mean. You don't need to be worried about air; that tends to be everywhere, although there was a rumour that, in the early seventies, Citroën investigated holding a car launch on the moon. They were thwarted by various things, one of which was undoubtedly Gallic laziness. Anyway, on the modern car launch, you will notice that, no sooner has the average journalist been bussed about, shoved into the car, hauled out of the car and shunted into the press conference, he is disappearing off to his room, not for what in the eighties Glen Gibly of The Cambridge Eye used to call the pre-dinner MAWAS (Minibar And a Wank And a Shower), but because he (or, worse yet, she) is required by the unreasonable strictures of the modern world to confect some thoughtless thoughts about the vehicle in question, all to satiate the endless appetites of that silly bitch, the internet. Quite frankly, the modern launch is very much like my third marriage, by which I mean hurried and annoying.

Amidst the unseemly events described above, the demand for instant prose is the one I find especially annoying and, though I now have a website of my own, I steadfastly refuse to rush my words simply to be the first, the fastest or the most accurate online. Nonetheless, it is a sad fact that the motor noting game has moved on and anyone wishing to get into it today will be well advised to consider the stress of having to write quickly and under great pressure, which, to my mind, is not what motoring journalism is all about and something that has to change sooner or later. I am certain I will eventually be proven correct on this one, assuming I stick around long enough to see it. Personally, I think I'll be fine, as long as my heart doesn't briefly stop on another Hyundai regional rotation in the East Midlands!

# 21. THE FUTURE

I wanted to end this book with a list of people in the motor industry who had annoyed and/or betrayed me, as an extension of the list I put on my website every December naming those who have died during the year and why I didn't like them. However, the publisher thought it would be more useful if, instead, I wrote a chapter looking at the future of both the car and motoring journalism itself. Reluctantly, I agreed.

The man who invented Honda once said that, in the future, there would be only six car companies plus Morgan, and, plainly, he was talking out of his arse. There are still loads of car companies around, all making excellent cars. However, I'm pleased to see Morgan on his list and not just because I got onto their stand at the recent Geneva Motor Show press day and drank a load of their whisky before they realised what was going on. I have never been able to enjoy Morgan's no-doubt excellent products on account of being too broad in the body and legs, but what I admire about their cars is how they eschew the fads of the modern world. This makes them immune to the idiotic whims of fashion and, I imagine, the law, as they carve their own furrow in a thoroughly British manner. It's unsurprising, for example, to see that Morgan were unaffected by the recent backlash against diesel, which, to my mind, was, and is, utterly ludicrous. I will admit that, for many years, I was a staunch opponent of diesel (or "diseasel" as I used to humourously call it, and did so many years before anyone else, I think). I regarded it as a filthy fuel powering chugging and unresponsive motors and not worth the bother unless you were doing thousands of miles a year in the same car which, thankfully, I was not. However, my mind was changed by some of the great advances made in diesel technology and, in particular, the excellent diesel engines offered by the Volkswagen Group in cars such as the Golf TDI. The economy figures from models like this were truly impressive, to the extent that you could drive one for a week and still be able to syphon a couple of cans of juice from the tank before it went back in order to keep for 'emergencies'. Yes, some of their vehicles later turned out to have irregularities in their emissions figures as a result of ingenious software modes, but if that is the price of greater smoothness, increased power and better economy, then so be it.

To my mind, the fault here actually lies with the needless meddling of governments and, in particular, the dreaded EU. Thanks to their draconian interference, car makers are being hamstrung in their quests to make diesel even better and, instead, are forced to fit idiotic systems such as diesel particulate filters (DPFs), which invariably go wrong over time. This is certainly the experience of my pal Kurt Burslam, who found his Mondeo minicab performing badly as a result of a knackered DPF. The cost to replace it was over £1000, so, on my advice, he had this wretched device removed entirely and found his car performing superbly thereafter, at least until it failed its MOT. He couldn't afford to fix it, the car had to be scrapped and he found himself without a livelihood. To my mind, yet another reason why Brexit can't come soon enough!

Going back to Morgan, the other thing I admire about their excellent cars is their simplicity. Each one comes with a steering wheel and three pedals and that's it (I presume). None of these so-called 'driver aids' for the masters of Malvern! To my mind, there is nothing wrong with doing the driving yourself; indeed, that is surely the point of a car? Computerised interference for the sake of it is just like having an electronic EU strapped to your car and, wherever possible, I will deploy 'digital Brexit', by which I mean setting all of these systems to 'goodbye' (i.e. off). If a pernickety press officer asks why the "lane assist warning stability braking assistance control system interference module" did not prevent the accident, I cheerfully tell them that understeering off the roundabout by Asda and smashing through an electricity sub-station was "the will of the people"!

Unfortunately, it seems that the motor industry, or, rather, the interfering ninnies of the PC brigade, want our cars to practically drive themselves in future and, worse yet, to be powered by electricity when doing so. I railed against this eco-nonsense when hybrids first came along and I will continue to burst the daft bubble of environ-mentalism as I see fit. Do not think, however, that I am some kind of foolish luddite, for that is plainly not the case. I am as fully aware of modern technology as the next man, as long as that man isn't David Scadley from The Belper Journal, who still calls emails "computer messages". He's got to be at least 80 now and, frankly, I'm amazed they still let him drive. I, on the other hand, am quite the modern man and would remind you that

I have a laptop computer, a mobile phone with a camera in it and that I ordered my last wife electronically. No, the modern world holds no surprises for me and, to that end, a couple of years ago, I thought I should see what all the fuss was about with electronic cars. As luck would have it, I knew the European PR man for an up-and-coming Taiwanish electro-mobile called the e-GO-E, which was being developed in co-operation with researchers at Central Midlands University in Leamington Spa (i.e. the Brits were doing all the complicated bits, I assume). As this PR chap owed me a favour for trying to dig him out of an expenses/whores hole with his former employer, I contacted him and insisted he lend me one of their pre-production demonstrators, as I knew for a fact they'd already let Mitch Skiller have a go in one and he basically has no outlets these days. He only goes on any launches he can for the food, which is pretty poor form in my book. The PR happily agreed that I could visit their R&D centre in the Midlands and I happily replied that this was too far away and that he would have to bring the car to my house, which, eventually, he agreed to do.

The e-GO-E or, to give its full name, the Aphos Dynamics e-GO-E Full Electric Vehicle System VM-series 4490M, was delivered the following week, along with the PR chap himself, who was rather too eager to explain the car's features to me, overlooking the fact that it was almost noon, I had already enjoyed a hearty slug of writing lubricant and was in no mood to watch, listen or stand up for any longer than necessary. Therefore, I shooed him away to the nearest bus stop, then grabbed the ample press pack and settled down with a refreshing glass of reading wine to see what was what. Unfortunately, the bumf turned out to be almost entirely in Taiwanish, which was rather a problem, since my knowledge of far eastern languages extends only to the sounds and facial expressions which have seen me barred from my local takeaway. Nonetheless, I was able to look with interest at some of the charts, graphs and diagrams, from which I learnt that the e-GO-E was up to 37 percent better at some things and boasted at least 96 out of 100 or maybe 10; it was quite hard to read. I also gathered with some interest that this model had a roof-mounted square that might have been a solar panel, some sort of thing in the boot that you should not touch and, more significantly, a self-driving capability. I resisted the temptation to tut at this point, as I was determinedly approaching this literature with an open mind/bottle.

The next morning, I was up early enough to have missed the end of the dreaded school run traffic and was looking forward to giving the e-GO-E a good test run. I recall noting that, from the outside, this machine resembled a smoothed out Renault Scenic, while behind the wheel, it was truly futuristic, by which I mean everything was white and confusing. However, I finally located the start button and gave it a firm press to be greeted not by engine noise but by a synthesized 'welcome' tone, which, I must confess, was so deep and flatulent that I briefly feared there had been a repeat of the reason why I got blacklisted by Nissan. With the dashboard now fully lit up in a Taiwanical manner, it was a mere five minutes until I located the thing that put the car into gear, after which I gave a gentle press on the throttle and drove smoothly into my own garage door. After a few minutes further study, I gave another twiddle on the gear selector knob and, with that, set off into the bloody garage door again. However, with no significant damage done to my property, and only a little to the car, I simply made a call to the PR man, got him to explain a couple of things and, after that, I reversed silently out onto the road and set off on my test drive.

As I said, I am no luddite and, though the case for electricity as a means of moving cars around is misguided and powered entirely by the kind of hand-wringing lefties that wouldn't know a good car if it was served to them in their lentil and hessian casserole, I will confess that I was impressed by the e-GO-E's strong torque and smooth, quiet running. Speed was gained without effort, roundabouts were approached with surprising speed, emergency braking efforts handled with stability, kerb strikes shrugged off almost completely. In fact, such was the extent to which I was reluctantly enjoying this Taiwanomanic machine that I hadn't noticed the rapid descent of the electric fuel gauge until I was startled by a strident honking noise that, once again, wasn't coming from me. Happily, I was just approaching the perfect electric car charging station, by which I mean The Black Lamb in Ramsdale, where the landlord was an old pal who would happily let me charge up at his pub, though, initially, he disagreed with both of those sentiments. After a bit of cajoling, Steve agreed to let me run a flex through the window of the ladies' toilets so that I could enjoy a relaxing late morning pint while the e-GO-E slurped on the electrical petrol we sometimes call electricity. This, of course, is the downside of this type of car and another reason why they will never take off, as there's only a double socket within cable stretching distance of the bog window at Steve's pub and how would that work if everyone turned up demanding to refuel electronically? He'd have to invest in a massive multi-plug extension lead and, frankly, I can't see him going for it, especially when any spare cash would be better spent on more pressing issues, such as the plumbing in the gents', which hasn't been right for ages and permanently gives off a very powerful aroma. If the future of motoring is a decision between lack of charging or a heavy smell of piss, I'll take the first option please.

The other huge issue with electric cars is something I soon discovered on my test drive of the e-GO-E, and that's the amount of time it takes to charge these things. Even after I had finished my third pint, the car was still barely 12 percent full, which is absurd when you remember that a petrol car would be topped to the brim in much less than those 40 minutes. However, all was not lost as I was just saying to Steve that my next pint would have to be my last since I was driving, when I remembered that the e-GO-E had a self-driving function. Finally, I could see some benefit to this modern technology. Of course, I would much rather do the driving myself, but I had to admit it was useful to know that I could now order another pint and some lunch and a couple of whisky chasers, secure in the knowledge that R2-P2 would be chauffeuring me home, safely and, presumably, legally.

Some time later, I instructed Steve to send the bill for the electricity, the lunch, the drinks and the broken window to the e-GO-E PR chap (jokingly adding that he should mark the envelope "prostitute receipts"), then settled back into my self-driving chariot and spent a mere 20 minutes working out how to put my home address into the sat nav. With that done, I carefully reversed into a low wall, then even more carefully backed out onto the road, put the car into 'drive', let it gain momentum down the hill out of the village and triumphantly removed my hands from the wheel.

I make no apologies for having mixed feelings about a car like the e-GO-E, but what I will say in its defence is that it was clearly well made and proved itself more than capable of surviving an impact caused by the driver's sudden realisation that his car isn't actually self-driving and, also, that he is going to be sick but can't work out which of the buttons puts the window down. As an aside, my experience with this pre-production car tells me that one can't discount the Taiwaners as a car-making nation of the future, although they would be advised to come up with some darker interior colour schemes and/or better vomit resistance.

Overall, I remain sceptical about electric vehicles and do not believe they are more than a passing fad, but, in many ways, I look forward to some cars offering a self-driving capability, as long as it doesn't interfere with the driver's role, unless he has been to the pub. Ultimately, however, I believe that the future of the car is much as it has always been; petrol or diesel powered, steel bodied, operated by a driver. After all, why mess with a winning formula? To prove my point, note that car sales frequently hit new highs these days, and that's without all this needless electrical power and autonomous technology that keeps being threatened. Clearly, the car makers are doing something right as it is. That's why I predict that these stupid fads will fall away in time and we will be left with careful evolution of the excellent cars we have today, and, of course, the professional experts who review them!

This last thought leads me naturally on to my next topic. With the future of the car dealt with, what of the future of motoring journalism? At the moment, it seems our industry is in the grip of two trends; the internet and, within that, the video reviewer (or 'vlogger'). Both are flavour of the month at the moment and have had some effect on the way the rest of us do our business. Car launches are now full of these online types flailing about with their video equipment and generally making a nuisance of themselves, while lacking even the good manners to stick around after dinner to enjoy the host manufacturer's hospitality in the bar and, perhaps later if you can bully the junior PR, titty club. This is just one of many reasons why I believe these people will not last the distance but, for now, I fear we have to put up with launches full of well-spoken children shouting "Hi there!" into their mobile phones.

We proper journalists must also accept that, sometimes these days, we will not make the launch invitation list without a huge argument because the press office claim all the places have been given to "influencers". Well let me tell you sunshine, I was "influencing" people with my proper, written car reviews back when these YouTubes idiots hadn't even managed to be born. Plus, just last year, I told Carol in the Harrogate Herald office to buy another Yaris and she did. If that's not having "influence", I don't know what is!

Lest you accuse me of hypocrisy, I am well aware that I too have a website and I will admit I've found Over The Limit With Roy Lanchester to be a very useful tool for keeping my hand in the game, not least because websites aren't subject to irritating independent readership audits. Plus, with a healthy audience of over 1100 unique reader view impressions per month, OTLWRL is clearly doing something right, despite my policy of refusing to chase readers, both literally and with instant new car reviews. Given the choice between rushing dinner on a launch and then running up to my room in an attempt to be first online with driving impressions or staying downstairs for more drinks and taking time to craft a more thoughtful review to be posted a few weeks later, you can guess which method I would choose. I'm confident that, over time, my approach will be proven to be correct. Moreover, I firmly believe that both 'vlogging' and the internet in general will be exposed as a fad and will die out as the young people of today realise how much of their lives they are wasting on nonsense like Snapchat and Friends Reunited.

The fact is, you simply cannot beat the simple pleasures of the written word and it's my view that anyone aspiring to enter motoring journalism now would do well to remember this and adjust their aim accordingly. It's just a matter of finding a magazine or newspaper that's still in business. Only print journalism can give the reader a quality and integrity that is so lacking in online videos and reports, and the world will come back to this just as it's come back to pies and proper brown beer and such.

That's why, to my mind, the future of motoring journalism is looking very bright, aside from a few petty niggles about money and relevance. Cars will continue to exist in their current form long into the future, and those cars will always need reviewing by people who know what they're talking about, such as yours truly. As long as that's the case, and as long as cars are still being launched in the proper way, you will find me there, in the car and, later, in the bar. For I am Roy Lanchester and I am a motoring journalist.

# ACKNOWLEDGEMENTS

Roy would like to thank Cyril Crest, Finnigan's Dry Cleaning of Harrogate, The Bottle Barn, Dean & Nick at The Red Lion, Pete at The Royal Oak, Karen and all at The King's Arms, Steve at The Black Lamb, Kenny, Johnny and all the good guys of PR, Richard Porter.

Sniff Petrol would like to thank Tom Barnard, Mark Bursa, Mankee Cheng, Jeremy Clarkson, Aaron Gold, Alex Goy, Simon Harris, Keith WR Jones, Ben Samuelson, James Warren, J, D & M.

Printed in Great Britain
by Amazon